Walt Whitman

Selected by
Ellman Crasnow

PHOENIX
POETRY

This edition first published in Everyman in 1996
Phoenix edition first published in 2002

Selection © J. M. Dent 1996
Chronology © J. M. Dent 2002

ISBN: 0 75381 666 0

Typeset by Deltatype Ltd,
Birkenhead, Merseyside
Printed in China by
South China Printing Co. Ltd.

A CIP catalogue reference for this book
is available from the British Library.

The Orion Publishing Group
Orion House
5 Upper St Martin's Lane
London
WC2H 9EA

Contents

Poems

Walt Whitman

There was a Child Went Forth

There was a child went forth every day,
And the first object he look'd upon, that object he
    became,
And that object became part of him for the day or a
    certain part of the day,
Or for many years or stretching cycles of years.

The early lilacs became part of this child,
And grass and white and red morning-glories, and
    white and red clover, and the song of the phoebe-
    bird,
And the Third-month lambs and the sow's pink-faint
    litter, and the mare's foal and the cow's calf,
And the noisy brood of the barnyard or by the mire of
    the pond-side,
And the fish suspending themselves so curiously below
    there, and the beautiful curious liquid,
And the water-plants with their graceful flat heads, all
    became part of him.

The field-sprouts of Fourth-month and Fifth-month
    became part of him,
Winter-grain sprouts and those of the light-yellow
    corn, and the esculent roots of the garden,
And the apple-trees cover'd with blossoms and the fruit
    afterward, and wood-berries, and the commonest
    weeds by the road.
And the old drunkard staggering home from the
    outhouse of the tavern whence he had lately risen,
And the schoolmistress that pass'd on her way to the
    school,

And the friendly boys that pass'd, and the quarrelsome
 boys,
And the tidy and fresh-cheek'd girls, and the barefoot
 negro boy and girl,
And all the changes of city and country wherever he
 went.

His own parents, he that had father'd him, and she
 that had conceiv'd him in her womb and birth'd
 him,
They gave this child more of themselves than that,
They gave him afterward every day, they became part
 of him.

The mother at home quietly placing the dishes on the
 supper-table,
The mother with mild words, clean her cap and gown,
 a wholesome odor falling off her person and clothes
 as she walks by,
The father, strong, self-sufficient, manly, mean,
 anger'd, unjust,
The blow, the quick loud word, the tight bargain, the
 crafty lure,
The family usages, the language, the company, the
 furniture, the yearning and swelling heart,
Affection that will not be gainsay'd, the sense of what
 is real, the thought if after all it should prove unreal,
The doubts of day-time and the doubts of night-time,
 the curious whether and how,
Whether that which appears so is so, or is it all flashes
 and specks?
Men and women crowding fast in the streets, if they
 are not flashes and specks what are they?

The streets themselves and the façades of houses, and goods in the windows,

Vehicles, teams, the heavy-plank'd wharves, the huge crossing at the ferries,

The village on the highland seen from afar at sunset, the river between,

Shadows, aureola and mist, the light falling on roofs and gables of white or brown two miles off,

The schooner near by sleepily dropping down the tide, the little boat slack-tow'd astern,

The hurrying tumbling waves, quick-broken crests, slapping,

The strata of color'd clouds, the long bar of maroon-tint away solitary by itself, the spread of purity it lies motionless in,

The horizon's edge, the flying sea-crow, the fragrance of salt marsh and shore mud,

These became part of that child who went forth every day, and who now goes, and will always go forth every day.

from Song of Myself

1

I celebrate myself, and sing myself,
And what I assume you shall assume,
For every atom belonging to me as good belongs to
  you.

I loafe and invite my soul,
I lean and loafe at my ease observing a spear of
  summer grass.

My tongue, every atom of my blood, form'd from this
  soil, this air,
Born here of parents born here from parents the same,
  and their parents the same,
I, now thirty-seven years old in perfect health begin,
Hoping to cease not till death.
Creeds and schools in abeyance,
Retiring back a while sufficed at what they are, but
  never forgotten,
I harbor for good or bad, I permit to speak at every
  hazard,
Nature without check with original energy.

2

Houses and rooms are full of perfumes, the shelves are
  crowded with perfumes,
I breathe the fragrance myself and know it and like it,
The distillation would intoxicate me also, but I shall
  not let it.

The atmosphere is not a perfume, it has no taste of the
  distillation, it is odorless,
It is for my mouth forever, I am in love with it,
I will go to the bank by the wood and become
  undisguised and naked,
I am mad for it to be in contact with me.
The smoke of my own breath,
Echoes, ripples, buzz'd whispers, love-root, silk-thread,
  crotch and vine,
My respiration and inspiration, the beating of my heart,
  the passing of blood and air through my lungs,
The sniff of green leaves and dry leaves, and of the
  shore and dark-color'd sea-rocks, and of hay in the
  barn,
The sound of the belch'd words of my voice loos'd to
  the eddies of the wind,
A few light kisses, a few embraces, a reaching around
  of arms,
The play of shine and shade on the trees as the supple
  boughs wag,
The delight alone or in the rush of the streets, or along
  the fields and hill-sides,
The feeling of health, the full-noon trill, the song of
  me rising from bed and meeting the sun.

Have you reckon'd a thousand acres much? have you
  reckon'd the earth much?
Have you practis'd so long to learn to read?
Have you felt so proud to get at the meaning of
  poems?

Stop this day and night with me and you shall possess
  the origin of all poems,

You shall possess the good of the earth and sun, (there
are millions of suns left,)
You shall no longer take things at second or third
hand, nor look through the eyes of the dead, nor
feed on the specters in books,
You shall not look through my eyes either, nor take
things from me,
You shall listen to all sides and filter them from your
self.

3

I have heard what the talkers were talking, the talk of
the beginning and the end,
But I do not talk of the beginning or the end.

There was never any more inception than there is now,
Nor any more youth or age than there is now,
And will never be any more perfection than there is
now,
Nor any more heaven or hell than there is now.

Urge and urge and urge,
Always the procreant urge of the world.
Out of the dimness opposite equals advance, always
substance and increase, always sex,
Always a knit of identity, always distinction, always a
breed of life.

To elaborate is no avail, learn'd and unlearn'd feel that
it is so.

Sure as the most certain sure, plumb in the uprights,
well entretied, braced in the beams,

Stout as a horse, affectionate, haughty, electrical,
I and this mystery here we stand.

Clear and sweet is my soul, and clear and sweet is all
    that is not my soul.

Lack one lacks both, and the unseen is proved by the
    seen,
Till that becomes unseen and receives proof in its turn.

Showing the best and dividing it from the worst age
    vexes age,
Knowing the perfect fitness and equanimity of things,
    while they discuss I am silent, and go bathe and
    admire myself.
Welcome is every organ and attribute of me, and of
    any man hearty and clean,
Not an inch nor a particle of an inch is vile, and none
    shall be less familiar than the rest.

I am satisfied – I see, dance, laugh, sing;
As the hugging and loving bed-fellow sleeps at my side
    through the night, and withdraws at the peep of the
    day with stealthy tread,
Leaving me baskets cover'd with white towels swelling
    the house with their plenty,
Shall I postpone my acceptation and realization and
    scream at my eyes,
That they turn from gazing after and down the road,
And forthwith cipher and show me to a cent,
Exactly the value of one and exactly the value of two,
    and which is ahead?

4

Trippers and askers surround me,
People I meet, the effect upon me of my early life or
    the ward and city I live in, or the nation,
The latest dates, discoveries, inventions, societies,
    authors old and new,
My dinner, dress, associates, looks, compliments, dues,
The real or fancied indifference of some man or
    woman I love,
The sickness of one of my folks or of myself, or ill-
    doing or loss or lack of money, or depressions or
    exaltations,
Battles, the horrors of fratricidal war, the fever of
    doubtful news, the fitful events;
These come to me days and nights and go from me
    again,
But they are not the Me myself.

Apart from the pulling and hauling stands what I am,
Stands amused, complacent, compassionating, idle,
    unitary,
Looks down, is erect, or bends an arm on an
    impalpable certain rest,
Looking with side-curved head curious what will come
    next,
Both in and out of the game and watching and
    wondering at it.

Backward I see in my own days where I sweated
    through fog with linguists and contenders,
I have no mockings or arguments, I witness and wait.

5

I believe in you my soul, the other I am must not
    abase itself to you,
And you must not be abased to the other,

Loafe with me on the grass, loose the stop from your
    throat,
Not words, not music or rhyme I want, not custom or
    lecture, not even the best,
Only the lull I like, the hum of your valvèd voice.

I mind how once we lay such a transparent summer
    morning,
How you settled your head athwart my hips and gently
    turn'd over upon me,
And parted the shirt from my bosom-bone, and
    plunged your tongue to my bare-stript heart,
And reach'd till you felt my beard, and reach'd till you
    held my feet.

Swiftly arose and spread around me the peace and
    knowledge that pass all the argument of the earth,
And I know that the hand of God is the promise of
    my own,
And I know that the spirit of God is the brother of my
    own,
And that all the men ever born are also my brothers,
    and the women my sisters and lovers,
And that a kelson of the creation is love,
And limitless are leaves stiff or drooping in the fields,
And brown ants in the little wells beneath them,
And mossy scabs of the worm fence, heap'd stones,
    elder, mullein and poke-weed.

6

A child said *What is the grass?* fetching it to me with full
    hands;
How could I answer the child? I do not know what it
    is any more than he.

I guess it must be the flag of my disposition, out of
    hopeful green stuff woven.
Or I guess it is the handkerchief of the Lord,
A scented gift and remembrancer designedly dropt,
Bearing the owner's name someway in the corners, that
    we may see and remark, and say *Whose?*

Or I guess the grass is itself a child, the produced babe
    of the vegetation.

Or I guess it is a uniform hieroglyphic,
And it means, Sprouting alike in broad zones and
    narrow zones,
Growing among black folks as among white,
Kanuck, Tuckahoe, Congressman, Cuff, I give them the
    same, I receive them the same.

And now it seems to me the beautiful uncut hair of
    graves.

Tenderly will I use you curling grass,
It may be you transpire from the breasts of young
    men,
It may be if I had known them I would have loved
    them,
It may be you are from old people, or from offspring
    taken soon out of their mothers' laps,
And here you are the mothers' laps.

This grass is very dark to be from the white heads of
    old mothers,
Darker than the colorless beards of old men,
Dark to come from under the faint red roofs of
    mouths.

O I perceive after all so many uttering tongues,
And I perceive they do not come from the roofs of
    mouths for nothing.

I wish I could translate the hints about the dead young
    men and women,
And the hints about old men and mothers, and the
    offspring taken soon out of their laps.

What do you think has become of the young and old
    men?
And what do you think has become of the women and
    children?

They are alive and well somewhere,
The smallest sprout shows there is really no death,
And if ever there was it led forward life, and does not
    wait at the end to arrest it,
And ceas'd the moment life appear'd.

All goes onward and outward, nothing collapses,
And to die is different from what any one supposed,
    and luckier.

7

Has any one supposed it lucky to be born?
I hasten to inform him or her it is just as lucky to die,
  and I know it.

I pass death with the dying and birth with the new-
  wash'd babe, and am not contain'd between my hat
  and boots,
And peruse manifold objects, no two alike and every
  one good,
The earth good and the stars good, and their adjuncts
  all good.

I am not an earth nor an adjunct of an earth,
I am the mate and companion of people, all just as
  immortal and fathomless as myself,
(They do not know how immortal, but I know.)

Every kind for itself and its own, for me mine male
  and female,
For me those that have been boys and that love
  women,
For me the man that is proud and feels how it stings
  to be slighted,
For me the sweet-heart and the old maid, for me
  mothers and the mothers of mothers,
For me lips that have smiled, eyes that have shed tears,
For me children and the begetters of children.

Undrape! you are not guilty to me, nor stale nor
  discarded,
I see through the broadcloth and gingham whether or
  no,

And am around, tenacious, acquisitive, tireless, and
  cannot be shaken away.

8

The little one sleeps in its cradle,
I lift the gauze and look a long time, and silently brush
  away flies with my hand.
The youngster and the red-faced girl turn aside up the
  busy hill,
I peeringly view them from the top.

The suicide sprawls on the bloody floor of the
  bedroom,
I witness the corpse with its dabbled hair, I note where
  the pistol has fallen.

The blab of the pave, tires of carts, sluff of boot-soles,
  talk of the promenaders,
The heavy omnibus, the driver with his interrogating
  thumb, the clank of the shod horses on the granite
  floor,
The snow-sleighs, clinking, shouted jokes, pelts of
  snow-balls,
The hurrahs for popular favorites, the fury of rous'd
  mobs,
The flap of the curtain'd litter, a sick man inside borne
  to the hospital,
The meeting of enemies, the sudden oath, the blows
  and fall,
The excited crowd, the policeman with his star quickly
  working his passage to the centre of the crowd,
The impassive stones that receive and return so many
  echoes,

What groans of over-fed or half-starv'd who fall
  sunstruck or in fits,
What exclamations of women taken suddenly who
  hurry home and give birth to babes,
What living and buried speech is always vibrating here,
  what howls restrain'd by decorum,
Arrests of criminals, slights, adulterous offers made,
  acceptances, rejections with convex lips,
I mind them or the show or resonance of them – I
  come and I depart.

11

Twenty-eight young men bathe by the shore,
Twenty-eight young men and all so friendly;
Twenty-eight years of womanly life and all so
  lonesome.

She owns the fine house by the rise of the bank,
She hides handsome and richly drest aft the blinds of
  the window.

Which of the young men does she like the best?
Ah the homeliest of them is beautiful to her.

Where are you off to, lady? for I see you,
You splash in the water there, yet stay stock still in
  your room.

Dancing and laughing along the beach came the
  twenty-ninth bather,
The rest did not see her, but she saw them and loved
  them.

The beards of the young men glisten'd with wet, it ran
    from their long hair,
Little streams pass'd all over their bodies.

An unseen hand also pass'd over their bodies,
It descended tremblingly from their temples and ribs.

The young men float on their backs, their white bellies
    bulge to the sun, they do not ask who seizes fast to
    them,
They do not know who puffs and declines with
    pendant and bending arch,
They do not think whom they souse with spray.

15

The pure contralto sings in the organ loft,
The carpenter dresses his plank, the tongue of his
    foreplane whistles its wild ascending lisp,
The married and unmarried children ride home to their
    Thanksgiving dinner,
The pilot seizes the king-pin, he heaves down with a
    strong arm,
The mate stands braced in the whale-boat, lance and
    harpoon are ready,
The duck-shooter walks by silent and cautious stretches,
The deacons are ordain'd with cross'd hands at the
    altar,
The spinning-girl retreats and advances to the hum of
    the big wheel,
The farmer stops by the bars as he walks on a First-day
    loafe and looks at the oats and rye,
The lunatic is carried at last to the asylum a confirm'd
    case,

(He will never sleep any more as he did in the cot in
   his mother's bedroom;)
The jour printer with gray head and gaunt jaws works
   at his case,
He turns his quid of tobacco while his eyes blurr with
   the manuscript;
The malform'd limbs are tied to the surgeon's table,
What is removed drops horribly in a pail;
The quadroon girl is sold at the auction-stand, the
   drunkard nods by the bar-room stove,
The machinist rolls up his sleeves, the policeman travels
   his beat, the gate-keeper marks who pass,
The young fellow drives the express-wagon, (I love
   him, though I do not know him;)
The half-breed straps on his light boots to compete in
   the race,
The western turkey-shooting draws old and young,
   some lean on their rifles, some sit on logs,
Out from the crowd steps the marksman, takes his
   position, levels his piece;
The groups of newly-come immigrants cover the wharf
   or levee,
As the woolly-pates hoe in the sugar-field, the overseer
   views them from his saddle,
The bugle calls in the ball-room, the gentlemen run for
   their partners, the dancers bow to each other,
The youth lies awake in the cedar-roof'd garret and
   harks to the musical rain,
The Wolverine sets traps on the creek that helps fill the
   Huron,
The squaw wrapt in her yellow-hemm'd cloth is
   offering moccasins and bead-bags for sale,
The connoisseur peers along the exhibition-gallery with
   half-shut eyes bent sideways,

As the deck-hands make fast the steamboat the plank is
   thrown for the shore-going passengers,
The young sister holds out the skein while the elder
   sister winds it off in a ball, and stops now and then
   for the knots,
The one-year wife is recovering and happy having a
   week ago borne her first child,
The clean-hair'd Yankee girl works with her sewing-
   machine or in the factory or mill,
The paving-man leans on his two-handed rammer, the
   reporter's lead flies swiftly over the note-book, the
   sign-painter is lettering with blue and gold,
The canal boy trots on the tow-path, the book-keeper
   counts at his desk, the shoemaker waxes his thread,
The conductor beats time for the band and all the
   performers follow him,
The child is baptized, the convert is making his first
   professions,
The regatta is spread on the bay, the race is begun,
   (how the white sails sparkle!)
The drover watching his drove sings out to them that
   would stray,
The pedler sweats with his pack on his back, (the
   purchaser higgling about the odd cent;)
The bride unrumples her white dress, the minute-hand
   of the clock moves slowly,
The opium-eater reclines with rigid head and just-
   open'd lips,
The prostitute draggles her shawl, her bonnet bobs on
   her tipsy and pimpled neck,
The crowd laugh at her blackguard oaths, the men jeer
   and wink to each other,
(Miserable! I do not laugh at your oaths nor jeer you;)

The President holding a cabinet council is surrounded
     by the great Secretaries,
On the piazza walk three matrons stately and friendly
     with twined arms,
The crew of the fish-smack pack repeated layers of
     halibut in the hold,
The Missourian crosses the plains toting his wares and
     his cattle,
As the fare-collector goes through the train he gives
     notice by the jingling of loose change,
The floor-men are laying the floor, the tinners are
     tinning the roof, the masons are calling for mortar,
In single file each shouldering his hod pass onward the
     laborers;
Seasons pursuing each other the indescribable crowd is
     gather'd, it is the fourth of Seventh-month, (what
     salutes of cannon and small arms!)
Seasons pursuing each other the plougher ploughs, the
     mower mows, the winter-grain falls in the ground;
Off on the lakes the pike-fisher watches and waits by
     the hole in the frozen surface,
The stumps stand thick round the clearing, the squatter
     strikes deep with his axe,
Flatboatmen make fast towards dusk near the cotton-
     wood or pecan-trees,
Coon-seekers go through the regions of the Red river
     or through those drain'd by the Tennessee, or
     through those of the Arkansas,
Torches shine in the dark that hangs on the
     Chattahooche or Altamahaw,
Patriarchs sit at supper with sons and grandsons and
     great-grandsons around them.
In walls of adobie, in canvas tents, rest hunters and
     trappers after their day's sport,

The city sleeps and the country sleeps,
The living sleep for their time, the dead sleep for their
time,
The old husband sleeps by his wife and the young
husband sleeps by his wife;
And these tend inward to me, and I tend outward to
them,
And such as it is to be of these more or less I am,
And of these one and all I weave the song of myself.

17

These are really the thoughts of all men in all ages and
lands, they are not original with me,
If they are not yours as much as mine they are
nothing, or next to nothing,
If they are not the riddle and the untying of the riddle
they are nothing,
If they are not just as close as they are distant they are
nothing.

This is the grass that grows wherever the land is and
the water is,
This is the common air that bathes the globe.

24

Walt Whitman, a kosmos, of Manhattan the son,
Turbulent, fleshy, sensual, eating, drinking and
breeding,
No sentimentalist, no stander above men and women
or apart from them,
No more modest than immodest.

Unscrew the locks from the doors!
Unscrew the doors themselves from their jambs!
Whoever degrades another degrades me,
And whatever is done or said returns at last to me.

Through me the afflatus surging and surging, through
    me the current and index.

I speak the pass-word primeval, I give the sign of
    democracy,
By God! I will accept nothing which all cannot have
    their counterpart of on the same terms.

Through me many long dumb voices,
Voices of the interminable generations of prisoners and
    slaves,
Voices of the diseas'd and despairing and of thieves
    and dwarfs,
Voices of cycles of preparation and accretion,
And of the threads that connect the stars, and of
    wombs and of the father-stuff,
And of the rights of them the others are down upon,
Of the deform'd, trivial, flat, foolish, despised,
Fog in the air, beetles rolling balls of dung.

Through me forbidden voices,
Voices of sexes and lusts, voices veil'd and I remove
    the veil,
Voices indecent by me clarified and transfigur'd.

I do not press my fingers across my mouth,
I keep as delicate around the bowels as around the
    head and heart,

Copulation is no more rank to me than death is.

I believe in the flesh and the appetites,
Seeing, hearing, feeling, are miracles, and each part and
    tag of me is a miracle.
Divine am I inside and out, and I make holy whatever
    I touch or am touch'd from,
The scent of these arm-pits aroma finer than prayer,
This head more than churches, bibles, and all the
    creeds.

If I worship one thing more than another it shall be
    the spread of my own body, or any part of it,
Translucent mould of me it shall be you!
Shaded ledges and rests it shall be you!
Firm masculine colter it shall be you!
Whatever goes to the tilth of me it shall be you!
You my rich blood! your milky stream pale strippings
    of my life!
Breast that presses against other breasts it shall be you!
My brain it shall be your occult convolutions!
Root of wash'd sweet-flag! timorous pond-snipe! nest
    of guarded duplicate eggs! it shall be you!
Mix'd tussled hay of head, beard, brawn, it shall be
    you!
Trickling sap of maple, fibre of manly wheat, it shall
    be you!
Sun so generous it shall be you!
Vapors lighting and shading my face it shall be you!
You sweaty brooks and dews it shall be you!
Winds whose soft-tickling genitals rub against me it
    shall be you!
Broad muscular fields, branches of live oak, loving
    lounger in my winding paths, it shall be you!

Hands I have taken, face I have kiss'd, mortal I have
  ever touch'd, it shall be you.

I dote on myself, there is that lot of me and all so
  luscious,
Each moment and whatever happens thrills me with
  joy,
I cannot tell how my ankles bend, nor whence the
  cause of my faintest wish,
Nor the cause of the friendship I emit, nor the cause
  of the friendship I take again.

That I walk up my stoop, I pause to consider if it
  really be,
A morning-glory at my window satisfies me more than
  the metaphysics of books.

To behold the day-break!
The little light fades the immense and diaphanous
  shadows,
The air tastes good to my palate.

Hefts of the moving world at innocent gambols silently
  rising, freshly exuding,
Scooting obliquely high and low.

Something I cannot see puts upward libidinous prongs,
Seas of bright juice suffuse heaven.
The earth by the sky staid with, the daily close of their
  junction,
The heav'd challenge from the east that moment over
  my head,

The mocking taunt, See then whether you shall be
master!

25

Dazzling and tremendous how quick the sun-rise would
kill me,
If I could not now and always send sun-rise out of me.

We also ascend dazzling and tremendous as the sun,
We found our own O my soul in the calm and cool of
the daybreak.

My voice goes after what my eyes cannot reach,
With the twirl of my tongue I encompass worlds and
volumes of worlds.

Speech is the twin of my vision, it is unequal to
measure itself,
It provokes me forever, it says sarcastically,
Walt you contain enough, why don't you let it out then?

Come now I will not be tantalized, you conceive too
much of articulation,
Do you not know O speech how the buds beneath you
are folded?
Waiting in gloom, protected by frost,
The dirt receding before my prophetical screams,
I underlying causes to balance them at last,
My knowledge my live parts, it keeping tally with the
meaning of all things,
Happiness, (which whoever hears me let him or her
set out in search of this day.)

My final merit I refuse you, I refuse putting from me
what I really am,

Encompass worlds, but never try to encompass me,
I crowd your sleekest and best by simply looking
toward you.

Writing and talk do not prove me,
I carry the plenum of proof and every thing else in my
face,
With the hush of my lips I wholly confound the
skeptic.

27

To be in any form, what is that?
(Round and round we go, all of us, and ever come
back thither,)
If nothing lay more develop'd the quahaug in its
callous shell were enough.

Mine is no callous shell,
I have instant conductors all over me whether I pass or
stop,
They seize every object and lead it harmlessly through
me.

I merely stir, press, feel with my fingers, and am
happy,
To touch my person to some one else's is about as
much as I can stand.

28

Is this then a touch? quivering me to a new identity,
Flames and ether making a rush for my veins,
Treacherous tip of me reaching and crowding to help
them,

My flesh and blood playing out lightning to strike what
    is hardly different from myself,
On all sides prurient provokers stiffening my limbs,
Straining the udder of my heart for its withheld drip,
Behaving licentious toward me, taking no denial,
Depriving me of my best as for a purpose,
Unbuttoning my clothes, holding me by the bare waist,
Deluding my confusion with the calm of the sunlight
    and pasture-fields,
Immodestly sliding the fellow-senses away,
They bribed to swap off with touch and go and graze
    at the edges of me,
No consideration, no regard for my draining strength
    or my anger,
Fetching the rest of the herd around to enjoy them a
    while,
Then all uniting to stand on a headland and worry me.

The sentries desert every other part of me,
They have left me helpless to a red marauder,
They all come to the headland to witness and assist
    against me.

I am given up by traitors,
I talk wildly, I have lost my wits, I and nobody else
    am the greatest traitor,
I went myself first to the headland, my own hands
    carried me there.

You villain touch! what are you doing? my breath is
    tight in its throat,
Unclench your floodgates, you are too much for me.

29

Blind loving wrestling touch, sheath'd hooded sharp-
tooth'd touch!
Did it make you ache so, leaving me?
Parting track'd by arriving, perpetual payment of
perpetual loan,
Rich showering rain, and recompense richer afterward.

Sprouts take and accumulate, stand by the curb prolific
and vital,
Landscapes projected masculine, full-sized and golden.

33

Space and Time! now I see it is true, what I guess'd at,
What I guess'd when I loaf'd on the grass,
What I guess'd while I lay alone in my bed,
And again as I walk'd the beach under the paling stars
of the morning.
My ties and ballasts leave me, my elbows rest in sea-
gaps,
I skirt sierras, my palms cover continents,
I am afoot with my vision.
By the city's quadrangular houses – in log huts,
camping with lumbermen,
Along the ruts of the turnpike, along the dry gulch and
rivulet bed,
Weeding my onion-patch or hoeing rows of carrots
and parsnips, crossing savannas, trailing in forests,
Prospecting, gold-digging, girdling the trees of a new
purchase,
Scorch'd ankle-deep by the hot sand, hauling my boat
down the shallow river,
Where the panther walks to and fro on a limb

overhead, where the buck turns furiously at the
hunter,
Where the rattlesnake suns his flabby length on a rock,
where the otter is feeding on fish,
Where the alligator in his tough pimples sleeps by the
bayou,
Where the black bear is searching for roots or honey,
where the beaver pats the mud with his paddle-
shaped tail;
Over the growing sugar, over the yellow-flower'd
cotton plant, over the rice in its low moist field,
Over the sharp-peak'd farm house, with its scallop'd
scum and slender shoots from the gutters,
Over the western persimmon, over the long-leav'd
corn, over the delicate blue-flower flax,
Over the white and brown buckwheat, a hummer and
buzzer there with the rest,
Over the dusky green of the rye as it ripples and
shades in the breeze;
Scaling mountains, pulling myself cautiously up,
holding on by low scragged limbs,
Walking the path worn in the grass and beat through
the leaves of the brush,
Where the quail is whistling betwixt the woods and
the wheat-lot,
Where the bat flies in the Seventh-month eve, where
the great gold-bug drops through the dark,
Where the brook puts out of the roots of the old tree
and flows to the meadow,
Where cattle stand and shake away flies with the
tremulous shuddering of their hides,
Where the cheese-cloth hangs in the kitchen, where
andirons straddle the hearth-slab, where cobwebs fall
in festoons from the rafters;

Where trip-hammers crash, where the press is whirling
its cylinders.
Where the human heart beats with terrible throes
under its ribs,
Where the pear-shaped balloon is floating aloft,
(floating in it myself and looking composedly
down,)
Where the life-car is drawn on the slip-noose, where
the heat hatches pale-green eggs in the dented sand,
Where the she-whale swims with her calf and never
forsakes it,
Where the steam-ship trails hind-ways its long pennant
of smoke,
Where the fin of the shark cuts like a black chip out of
the water,
Where the half-burn'd brig is riding on unknown
currents,
Where shells grow to her slimy deck, where the dead
are corrupting below;
Where the dense-starr'd flag is borne at the head of the
regiments,
Approaching Manhattan up by the long-stretching
island,
Under Niagara, the cataract falling like a veil over my
countenance,
Upon a door-step, upon the horse-block of hard wood
outside,
Upon the race-course, or enjoying picnics or jigs or a
good game of base-ball,
At he-festivals, with blackguard gibes, ironical license,
bull-dances, drinking, laughter,
At the cider-mill tasting the streets of the brown mash,
sucking the juice through a straw,

At apple-peelings wanting kisses for all the red fruit I
find,
At musters, beach-parties, friendly bees, huskings,
house-raisings;
Where the mocking-bird sounds his delicious gurgles,
cackles, screams, weeps,
Where the hay-rick stands in the barn-yard, where the
dry-stalks are scatter'd, where the brood-cow waits
in the hovel,
Where the bull advances to do his masculine work,
where the stud to the mare, where the cock is
treading the hen,
Where the heifers browse, where geese nip their food
with short jerks,
Where sun-down shadows lengthen over the limitless
and lonesome prairie,
Where herds of buffalo make a crawling spread of the
square miles far and near,
Where the humming-bird shimmers, where the neck of
the long-lived swan is curving and winding,
Where the laughing-gull scoots by the shore, where
she laughs her near-human laugh,
Where bee-hives range on a gray bench in the garden
half hid by the high weeds,
Where band-neck'd partridges roost in a ring on the
ground with their heads out,
Where burial coaches enter the arch'd gates of a
cemetery,
Where winter wolves bark amid wastes of snow and
icicled trees,
Where the yellow-crown'd heron comes to the edge of
the marsh at night and feeds upon small crabs,
Where the splash of swimmers and divers cools the
warm noon,

Where the katy-did works her chromatic reed on the
walnut-tree over the well,

Through patches of citrons and cucumbers with silver-
wired leaves,

Through the salt-lick or orange glade, or under conical
firs,

Through the gymnasium, through the curtain'd saloon,
through the office or public hall;

Pleas'd with the native and pleas'd with the foreign,
pleas'd with the new and old,

Pleas'd with the homely woman as well as the
handsome,

Pleas'd with the quakeress as she puts off her bonnet
and talks melodiously,

Pleas'd with the tune of the choir of the whitewash'd
church,

Pleas'd with the earnest words of the sweating
Methodist preacher, impress'd seriously at the camp-
meeting;

Looking in at the shop-windows of Broadway the
whole forenoon, flatting the flesh of my nose on the
thick plate glass,

Wandering the same afternoon with my face turn'd up
to the clouds, or down a lane or along the beach,

My right and left arms round the sides of two friends,
and I in the middle;

Coming home with the silent and dark-cheek'd bush-
boy, (behind me he rides at the drape of the day,)

Far from the settlements studying the print of animals'
feet, or the moccasin print,

By the cot in the hospital reaching lemonade to a
feverish patient,

Nigh the coffin'd corpse when all is still, examining
with a candle;

Voyaging to every port to dicker and adventure,
Hurrying with the modern crowd as eager and flickle
as any,
Hot toward one I hate, ready in my madness to knife
him,
Solitary at midnight in my back yard, my thoughts
gone from me a long while,
Walking the old hills of Judaea with the beautiful
gentle God by my side,
Speeding through space, speeding through heaven and
the stars,
Speeding amid the seven satellites and the broad ring,
and the diameter of eighty thousand miles,
Speeding with tail'd meteors, throwing fire-balls like
the rest,
Carrying the crescent child that carries its own full
mother in its belly,
Storming, enjoying, planning, loving, cautioning,
Backing and filling, appearing and disappearing,
I tread day and night such roads.

I visit the orchards of spheres and look at the product,
And look at quintillions ripen'd and look at quintillions
green.

I fly those flights of a fluid and swallowing soul,
My course runs below the soundings of plummets.

I help myself to material and immaterial,
No guard can shut me off, no law prevent me.

I anchor my ship for a little while only,
My messengers continually cruise away or bring their
returns to me.

I go hunting polar furs and the seal, leaping chasms
    with a pike-pointed staff, clinging to topples of
    brittle and blue.

I ascend to the foretruck,
I take my place late at night in the crow's-nest,
We sail the arctic sea, it is plenty light enough,
Through the clear atmosphere I stretch around on the
    wonderful beauty,
The enormous masses of ice pass me and I pass them,
    the scenery is plain in all directions,
The white-topt mountains show in the distance, I fling
    out my fancies toward them,
We are approaching some great battle-field in which
    we are soon to be engaged,
We pass the colossal outposts of the encampment, we
    pass with still feet and caution,
Or we are entering by the suburbs some vast and
    ruin'd city,
The blocks and fallen architecture more than all the
    living cities of the globe.

I am a free companion, I bivouac by invading
    watchfires,
I turn the bridegroom out of bed and stay with the
    bride myself,
I tighten her all night to my thighs and lips.

My voice is the wife's voice, the screech by the rail of
    the stairs,
They fetch my man's body up dripping and drown'd.

I understand the large hearts of heroes,
The courage of present times and all times,

How the skipper saw the crowded and rudderless
    wreck of the steam-ship, and Death chasing it up
    and down the storm,
How he knuckled tight and gave not back an inch, and
    was faithful of days and faithful of nights,
And chalk'd in large letters on a board, *Be of good cheer,*
    we will not desert you;
How he follow'd with them and tack'd with them
    three days and would not give it up,
How he saved the drifting company at last,
How the lank loose-gown'd women look'd when
    boated from the side of their prepared graves,
How the silent old-faced infants and the lifted sick, and
    the sharp-lipp'd unshaved men;
All this I swallow, it tastes good, I like it well, it
    becomes mine,
I am the man, I suffer'd, I was there.

The disdain and calmness of martyrs,
The mother of old, condemn'd for a witch, burnt with
    dry wood, her children gazing on,
The hounded slave that flags in the race, leans by the
    fence, blowing, cover'd with sweat,
The twinges that sting like needles his legs and neck,
    the murderous buckshot and the bullets,
All these I feel or am.

I am the hounded slave, I wince at the bite of the
    dogs,
Hell and despair are upon me, crack and again crack
    the marksmen,
I clutch the rails of the fence, my gore dribs, thinn'd
    with the ooze of my skin,
I fall on the weeds and stones,

The riders spur their unwilling horses, haul close,
Taunt my dizzy ears and beat me violently over the
 head with whipstocks.

Agonies are one of my changes of garments,
I do not ask the wounded person how he feels, I
 myself become the wounded person,
My hurts turn livid upon me as I lean on a cane and
 observe.

I am the mash'd fireman with breast-bone broken,
Tumbling walls buried me in their debris,
Heat and smoke I inspired, I heard the yelling shouts
 of my comrades,
I heard the distant click of their picks and shovels,
They have clear'd the beams away, they tenderly lift
 me forth.
I lie in the night air in my red shirt, the pervading
 hush is for my sake,
Painless after all I lie exhausted but not so unhappy,
White and beautiful are the faces around me, the heads
 are bared of their fire-caps,
The kneeling crowd fades with the light of the torches.
Distant and dead resuscitate,
They show as the dial or move as the hands of me, I
 am the clock myself.

I am an old artillerist, I tell of my fort's bombardment,
I am there again.
Again the long roll of the drummers,
Again the attacking cannon, mortars,
Again to my listening ears the cannon responsive.

I take part, I see and hear the whole,

The cries, curses, roar, the plaudits for well-aim'd
    shots,
The ambulanza slowly passing trailing its red drip,
Workmen searching after damages, making
    indispensable repairs,
The fall of grenades through the rent roof, the fan-
    shaped explosion,
The whizz of limbs, heads, stone, wood, iron, high in
    the air.

Again gurgles the mouth of my dying general, he
    furiously waves with his hand.
He gasps through the clot *Mind not me — mind — the*
entrenchments.

48

I have said that the soul is not more than the body,
And I have said that the body is not more than the
    soul,
And nothing, not God, is greater to one than one's self
    is,
And whoever walks a furlong without sympathy walks
    to his own funeral drest in his shroud,
And I or you pocketless of a dime may purchase the
    pick of the earth,
And to glance with an eye or show a bean in its pod
    confounds the learning of all times,
And there is no trade or employment but the young
    man following it may become a hero,
And there is no object so soft but it makes a hub for
    the wheel'd universe,
And I say to any man or woman, Let your soul stand
    cool and composed before a million universes.

And I say to mankind, Be not curious about God,
For I who am curious about each am not curious about
  God,
(No array of terms can say how much I am at peace
  about God and about death.)

I hear and behold God in every object, yet understand
  God not in the least,
Nor do I understand who there can be more wonderful
  than myself.
Why should I wish to see God better than this day?
I see something of God each hour of the twenty-four,
  and each moment then,
In the faces of men and women I see God, and in my
  own face in the glass,
I find letters from God dropt in the street, and every
  one is sign'd by God's name,
And I leave them where they are, for I know that
  wheresoe'er I go,
Others will punctually come for ever and ever.

49

And as to you, Death, and you bitter hug of mortality,
  it is idle to try to alarm me.

To his work without flinching the accoucheur comes,
I see the elder-hand pressing receiving supporting,
I recline by the sills of the exquisite flexible doors,
And mark the outlet, and mark the relief and escape.

And as to you Corpse I think you are good manure,
  but that does not offend me,
I smell the white roses sweet-scented and growing,

I reach to the leafy lips, I reach to the polish'd breasts
of melons.
And as to you Life I reckon you are the leavings of
many deaths,
(No doubt I have died myself ten thousand times
before.)

I hear you whispering there O stars of heaven,
O suns – O grass of graves – O perpetual transfers and
promotions,
If you do not say any thing how can I say any thing?

Of the turbid pool that lies in the autumn forest,
Of the moon that descends the steeps of the soughing
twilight,
Toss, sparkles of day and dusk – toss on the black
stems that decay in the muck,
Toss to the moaning gibberish of the dry limbs.
I ascend from the moon, I ascend from the night,
I perceive that the ghastly glimmer is noonday
sunbeams reflected,
And debouch to the steady and central from the
offspring great or small.

50

There is that in me – I do not know what it is – but I
know it is in me.

Wrench'd and sweaty – calm and cool then my body
becomes,
I sleep – I sleep long.

I do not know it – it is without name – it is a word
unsaid,

It is not in any dictionary, utterance, symbol.

Something it swings on more than the earth I swing
    on,
To it the creation is the friend whose embracing
    awakes me.

Perhaps I might tell more. Outlines! I plead for my
    brothers and sisters.

Do you see O my brothers and sisters?
It is not chaos or death — it is form, union, plan — it is
    eternal life — it is Happiness.

51

The past and present wilt — I have fill'd them, emptied
    them,
And proceed to fill my next fold of the future.
Listener up there! what have you to confide to me?
Look in my face while I snuff the sidle of evening,
(Talk honestly, no one else hears you, and I stay only
    a minute longer.)

Do I contradict myself?
Very well then I contradict myself,
(I am large, I contain multitudes.)

I concentrate toward them that are nigh, I wait on the
    door-slab.
Who has done his day's work? who will soonest be
    through with his supper?
Who wishes to walk with me?

Will you speak before I am gone? will you prove
    already too late?

52

The spotted hawk swoops by and accuses me, he
    complains of my gab and my loitering.

I too am not a bit tamed, I too am untranslatable,
I sound my barbaric yawp over the roofs of the world.

The last scud of day holds back for me,
It flings my likeness after the rest and true as any on
    the shadow'd wilds,
It coaxes me to the vapor and the dusk.

I depart as air, I shake my white locks at the runaway
    sun,
I effuse my flesh in eddies, and drift it in lacy jags.

I bequeath myself to the dirt to grow from the grass I
    love,
If you want me again look for me under your boot-
    soles.

You will hardly know who I am or what I mean,
But I shall be good health to you nevertheless,
And filter and fibre your blood.

Failing to fetch me at first keep encouraged,
Missing me one place search another,
I stop somewhere waiting for you.

A Song for Occupations

I

A song for occupations!
In the labor of engines and trades and the labor of
    fields I find the developments,
And find the eternal meanings.

Workmen and Workwomen!
Were all educations practical and ornamental well
    display'd out of me, what would it amount to?
Were I as the head teacher, charitable proprietor, wise
    statesman, what would it amount to?
Were I to you as the boss employing and paying you,
    would that satisfy you?

The learn'd, virtuous, benevolent, and the usual terms,
A man like me and never the usual terms.

Neither a servant nor a master I,
I take no sooner a large price than a small price, I will
    have my own whoever enjoys me,
I will be even with you and you shall be even with
    me.

If you stand at work in a shop I stand as nigh as the
    nighest in the same shop,
If you bestow gifts on your brother or dearest friend I
    demand as good as your brother or dearest friend,
If your lover, husband, wife, is welcome by day or
    night, I must be personally as welcome,

If you become degraded, criminal, ill, then I become
  so for your sake,
If you remember your foolish and outlaw'd deeds, do
  you think I cannot remember my own foolish and
  outlaw'd deeds?
If you carouse at the table I carouse at the opposite
  side of the table,
If you meet some stranger in the streets and love him
  or her, why I often meet strangers in the street and
  love them.

Why what have you thought of yourself?
Is it you then that thought yourself less?
Is it you that thought the President greater than you?
Or the rich better off than you? or the educated wiser
  than you?
(Because you are greasy or pimpled, or were once
  drunk, or a thief,
Or that you are diseas'd, or rheumatic, or a prostitute,
Or from frivolity or impotence, or that you are no
  scholar and never saw your name in print,
Do you give in that you are any less immortal?)

2

Souls of men and women! it is not you I call unseen,
  unheard, untouchable and untouching,
It is not you I go argue pro and con about, and to
  settle whether you are alive or no,
I own publicly who you are, if nobody else owns.

Grown, half-grown and babe, of this country and every
  country, indoors, and out-doors, one just as much as
  the other, I see,
And all else behind or through them.

The wife, and she is not one jot less than the husband,
The daughter, and she is just as good as the son,
The mother, and she is every bit as much as the father.

Offspring of ignorant and poor, boys apprenticed to
  trades,
Young fellows working on farms and old fellows
  working on farms,
Sailor-men, merchant-men, coasters, immigrants,
All these I see, but nigher and farther the same I see,
None shall escape me and none shall wish to escape
  me.

I bring what you much need yet always have,
Not money, amours, dress, eating, erudition, but as
  good,
I send no agent or medium, offer no representative of
  value, but offer the value itself.

There is something that comes to one now and
  perpetually,
It is not what is printed, preach'd, discussed, it eludes
  discussion and print,
It is not to be put in a book, it is not in this book,
It is for you whoever you are, it is no farther from
  you than your hearing and sight are from you,
It is hinted by nearest, commonest, readiest, it is ever
  provoked by them.
You may read in many languages, yet read nothing
  about it,
You may read the President's message and read nothing
  about it there,
Nothing in the reports from the State department or
  Treasury department, or in the daily papers or
  weekly papers,

Or in the census or revenue returns, prices current, or
  any accounts of stock.

3

The sun and stars that float in the open air,
The apple-shaped earth and we upon it, surely the drift
  of them is something grand,
I do not know what it is except that it is grand, and
  that it is happiness,
And that the enclosing purport of us here is not a
  speculation or bon-mot or reconnoissance,
And that it is not something which by luck may turn
  out well for us, and without luck must be a failure
  for us,
And not something which may yet be retracted in a
  certain contingency.

The light and shade, the curious sense of body and
  identity, the greed that with perfect complaisance
  devours all things,
The endless pride and outstretching of man,
  unspeakable joys and sorrows,
The wonder every one sees in every one else he sees,
  and the wonders that fill each minute of time
  forever,
What have you reckon'd them for, camerado?
Have you reckon'd them for your trade or farm-work?
  or for the profits of your store?
Or to achieve yourself a position? or to fill a
  gentleman's leisure, or a lady's leisure?

Have you reckon'd that the landscape took substance

and form that it might be painted in a picture?

Or men and women that they might be written of, and songs sung?

Or the attraction of gravity, and the great laws and harmonious combinations and the fluids of the air, as subjects for the savans?

Or the brown land and the blue sea for maps and charts?

Or the stars to be put in constellations and named fancy names?

Or that the growth of seeds is for agricultural tables, or agriculture itself?

Old institutions, these arts, libraries, legends, collections, and the practice handed along in manufactures, will we rate them so high?

Will we rate our cash and business high? I have no objection,

I rate them as high as the highest – then a child born of a woman and man I rate beyond all rate.

We thought our Union grand, and our Constitution grand,

I do not say they are not grand and good, for they are,

I am this day just as much in love with them as you,

Then I am in love with You, and with all my fellows upon the earth.

We consider bibles and religions divine – I do not say they are not divine,

I say they have all grown out of you, and may grow out of you still,

It is not they who give the life, it is you who give the life,

Leaves are not more shed from the trees, or trees from
the earth, than they are shed out of you.

4

The sum of all known reverence I add up in you
whoever you are,
The President is there in the White House for you, it is
not you who are here for him,
The Secretaries act in their bureaus for you, not you
here for them,
The Congress convenes every Twelfth-month for you,
Laws, courts, the forming of States, the charters of
cities, the going and coming of commerce and
mails, are all for you.

List close my scholars dear,
Doctrines, politics and civilization exurge from you,
Sculpture and monuments and any thing inscribed
anywhere are tallied in you,
The gist of histories and statistics as far back as the
records reach is in you this hour, and myths and
tales the same,
If you were not breathing and walking here, where
would they all be?
The most renown'd poems would be ashes, orations
and plays would be vacuums.

All architecture is what you do to it when you look
upon it,
(Did you think it was in the white or gray stone? or
the lines of the arches and cornices?)
All music is what awakes from you when you are
reminded by the instruments,

It is not the violins and the cornets, it is not the oboe
    nor the beating drums, nor the score of the baritone
    singer singing his sweet romanza, nor that of the
    men's chorus, nor that of the women's chorus.
It is nearer and farther than they.

5

Will the whole come back then?
Can each see signs of the best by a look in the
    looking-glass? is there nothing greater or more?
Does all sit there with you, with the mystic unseen
    soul?

Strange and hard that paradox true I give,
Objects gross and the unseen soul are one.

House-building, measuring, sawing the boards,
Blacksmithing, glass-blowing, nail-making, coopering,
    tin-roofing, shingle-dressing,
Ship-joining, dock-building, fish-curing, flagging of
    side-walks by flaggers,
The pump, the pile-driver, the great derrick, the coal-
    kiln and brick-kiln,
Coal-mines and all that is down there, the lamps in the
    darkness, echoes, songs, what meditations, what vast
    native thoughts looking through smutch'd faces,
Iron-works, forge-fires in the mountains or by river-
    banks, men around feeling the melt with huge
    crowbars, lumps of ore, the due combining of ore,
    limestone, coal,
The blast-furnace and the pudding-furnace, the loup-
    lump at the bottom of the melt at last, the rolling-

mill, the stumpy bars of pig-iron, the strong, clean-
shaped T-rail for railroads.

Oil-works, silk-works, white-lead-works, the sugar-
house, steam-saws, the great mills and factories,

Stone-cutting, shapely trimmings for façades or window
or door-lintels, the mallet, the tooth-chisel, the jib to
protect the thumb,

The calking-iron, the kettle of boiling vault-cement,
and the fire under the kettle,

The cotton-bale, the stevedore's hook, the saw and
buck of the sawyer, the mould of the moulder, the
working-knife of the butcher, the ice-saw, and all
the work with ice,

The work and tools of the rigger, grappler, sail-maker,
block-maker,

Goods of gutta-percha, papier-maché, colors, brushes,
brush-making, glazier's implements,

The veneer and glue-pot, the confectioner's ornaments,
the decanter and glasses, the shears and flat-iron,

The awl and knee-strap, the pint measure and quart
measure, the counter and stool, the writing-pen of
quill or metal, the making of all sorts of edged
tools,

The brewery, brewing, the malt, the vats, everything
that is done by brewers, wine-makers, vinegar-
makers,

Leather-dressing, coach-making, boiler-making, rope-
twisting, distilling, sign-painting, lime-burning,
cotton-picking, electroplating, electrotyping,
stereotyping,

Stave-machines, planing-machines, reaping-machines,
ploughing-machines, thrashing-machines, steam
wagons,

The cart of the carman, the omnibus, the ponderous
   dray,
Pyrotechny, letting off color'd fireworks at night, fancy
   figures and jets;
Beef on the butcher's stall, the slaughter-house of the
   butcher, the butcher in his killing-clothes,
The pens of live pork, the killing-hammer, the hog-
   hook, the scalder's tub, gutting, the cutter's cleaver,
   the packer's maul, and the plenteous winterwork of
   pork-packing,
Flour-works, grinding of wheat, rye, maize, rice, the
   barrels and the half and quarter barrels, the loaded
   barges, the high piles on wharves and levees,
The men and the work of the men on ferries,
   railroads, coasters, fish-boats, canals;
The hourly routine of your own or any man's life, the
   shop, yard, store, or factory,
These shows all near you by day and night –
   workman! whoever you are, your daily life!
In that and them the heft of the heaviest – in that and
   them far more than you estimated, (and far less
   also,)
In them realities for you and me, in them poems for
   you and me,
In them, not yourself – you and your soul enclose all
   things, regardless of estimation,
In them the development good – in them all themes,
   hints, possibilities.

I do not affirm that what you see beyond is futile, I
   do not advise you to stop,
I do not say leadings you thought great are not great,
But I say that none lead to greater than these lead to.

6

Will you seek afar off? you surely come back at last,
In things best known to you finding the best, or as
    good as the best,
In folks nearest to you finding the sweetest, strongest,
    lovingest,
Happiness, knowledge, not in another place but this
    place, not for another hour but this hour,
Man in the first you see or touch, always in friend,
    brother, nighest neighbor — woman in mother,
    sister, wife,
The popular tastes and employments taking precedence
    in poems or anywhere,
You workwomen and workmen of these States having
    your own divine and strong life,
And all else giving place to men and women like you.

When the psalm sings instead of the singer,
When the script preaches instead of the preacher,
When the pulpit descends and goes instead of the
    carver that carved the supporting desk,
When I can touch the body of books by night or by
    day, and when they touch my body back again,
When a university course convinces like a slumbering
    woman and child convince,
When the minted gold in the vault smiles like the
    night-watchman's daughter,
When warrantee deeds loafe in chairs opposite and are
    my friendly companions,
I intend to reach them my hand, and make as much of
    them as I do of men and women like you.

The Sleepers

I

I wander all night in my vision,
Stepping with light feet, swiftly and noiselessly
    stepping and stopping,
Bending with open eyes over the shut eyes of sleepers,
Wandering and confused, lost to myself, ill-assorted,
    contradictory,
Pausing, gazing, bending, and stopping.
How solemn they look there, stretch'd and still,
How quiet they breathe, the little children in their
    cradles.

The wretched features of ennuyés, the white features of
    corpses, the livid faces of drunkards, the sick-gray
    faces of onanists,
The gash'd bodies on battle-fields, the insane in their
    strong-door'd rooms, the sacred idiots, the new-born
    emerging from gates, and the dying emerging from
    gates,
The night pervades them and infolds them.

The married couple sleep calmly in their bed, he with
    his palm on the hip of the wife, and she with her
    palm on the hip of the husband,
The sisters sleep lovingly side by side in their bed,
The men sleep lovingly side by side in theirs,
And the mother sleeps with her little child carefully
    wrapt.

The blind sleep, and the deaf and dumb sleep,

The prisoner sleeps well in the prison, the runaway son
    sleeps,
The murderer that is to be hung next day, how does
    he sleep?
And the murder'd person, how does he sleep?

The female that loves unrequited sleeps,
And the male that loves unrequited sleeps,
The head of the money-maker that plotted all day
    sleeps,
And the enraged and treacherous dispositions, all, all
    sleep.

I stand in the dark with drooping eyes by the worst-
    suffering and the most restless,
I pass my hands soothingly to and fro a few inches
    from them,
The restless sink in their beds, they fitfully sleep.
Now I pierce the darkness, new beings appear,
The earth recedes from me into the night,
I saw that it was beautiful, and I see that what is not
    the earth is beautiful.

I go from bedside to bedside, I sleep close with the
    other sleepers each in turn,
I dream in my dream all the dreams of the other
    dreamers,
And I become the other dreamers.

I am a dance – play up there! the fit is whirling me
    fast!
I am the ever-laughing – it is new moon and twilight,
I see the hiding of douceurs, I see nimble ghosts
    whichever way I look,

Cache and cache again deep in the ground and sea, and
where it is neither ground nor sea.

Well do they do their jobs those journeymen divine,
Only from me can they hide nothing, and would not if
they could,
I reckon I am their boss and they make me a pet
besides,
And surround me and lead me and run ahead when I
walk,
To lift their cunning covers to signify me with
stretch'd arms, and resume the way;
Onward we move, a gay gang of blackguards! with
mirth-shouting music and wild-flapping pennants of
joy!

I am the actor, the actress, the voter, the politician,
The emigrant and the exile, the criminal that stood in
the box,
He who has been famous and he who shall be famous
after today,
The stammerer, the well-formed person, the wasted or
feeble person.
I am she who adorn'd herself and folded her hair
expectantly,
My truant lover has come, and it is dark.

Double yourself and receive me darkness,
Receive me and my lover too, he will not let me go
without him.

I roll myself upon you as upon a bed, I resign myself
to the dusk.

He whom I call answers me and takes the place of my
    lover,
He rises with me silently from the bed.

Darkness, you are gentler than my lover, his flesh was
    sweaty and panting,
I feel the hot moisture yet that he left me.

My hands are spread forth, I pass them in all
    directions,
I would sound up the shadowy shore to which you are
    journeying.

Be careful darkness! already what was it touch'd me?
I thought my lover had gone, else darkness and he are
    one,
I hear the heart-beat, I follow, I fade away.

2

I descend my western course, my sinews are flaccid,
Perfume and youth course through me and I am their
    wake.

It is my face yellow and wrinkled instead of the old
    woman's,
I sit low in a straw-bottom chair and carefully darn my
    grandson's stockings.

It is I too, the sleepless widow looking out on the
    winter midnight,
I see the sparkles of starshine on the icy and pallid
    earth.

A shroud I see and I am the shroud, I wrap a body
and lie in the coffin,
It is dark here under ground, it is not evil or pain
here, it is blank here, for reasons.

(It seems to me that every thing in the light and air
ought to be happy,
Whoever is not in his coffin and the dark grave let
him know he has enough.)

3

I see a beautiful gigantic swimmer swimming naked
through the eddies of the sea,
His brown hair lies close and even to his head, he
strikes out with courageous arms, he urges himself
with his legs,
I see his white body, I see his undaunted eyes,
I hate the swift-running eddies that would dash him
head-foremost on the rocks.

What are you doing you ruffianly red-trickled waves?
Will you kill the courageous giant? will you kill him in
the prime of his middle age?

Steady and long he struggles,
He is baffled, bang'd, bruis'd, he holds out while his
strength holds out,
The slapping eddies are spotted with his blood, they
bear him away, they roll him, swing him, turn him,
His beautiful body is borne in the circling eddies, it is
continually bruis'd on rocks,
Swiftly and out of sight is borne the brave corpse.

4

I turn but do not extricate myself,
Confused, a past-reading, another, but with darkness
    yet.

The beach is cut by the razory ice-wind, the wreck-
    guns sound,
The tempest lulls, the moon comes floundering through
    the drifts.

I look where the ship helplessly heads end on, I hear
    the burst as she strikes, I hear the howls of dismay,
    they grow fainter and fainter.

I cannot aid with my wringing fingers,
I can but rush to the surf and let it drench me and
    freeze upon me.

I search with the crowd, not one of the company is
    wash'd to us alive,
In the morning I help pick up the dead and lay them
    in rows in a barn.

5

Now of the older war-days, the defeat at Brooklyn,
Washington stands inside the lines, he stands on the
    intrench'd hills amid a crowd of officers,
His face is cold and damp, he cannot repress the
    weeping drops,
He lifts the glass perpetually to his eyes, the color is
    blanch'd from his cheeks,

He sees the slaughter of the southern braves confided
    to him by their parents.

The same at last and at last when peace is declared,
He stands in the room of the old tavern, the well-
    belov'd soldiers all pass through,
The officers speechless and slow draw near in their
    turns,
The chief encircles their necks with his arm and kisses
    them on the cheek,
He kisses lightly the wet-cheeks one after another, he
    shakes hands and bids good-by to the army.

6

Now what my mother told me one day as we sat at
    dinner together,
Of when she was a nearly grown girl living home with
    her parents on the old homestead.

A red squaw came one breakfast-time to the old
    homestead,
On her back she carried a bundle of rushes for rush-
    bottoming chairs,
Her hair, straight, shiny, coarse, black, profuse, half-
    envelop'd her face,
Her step was free and elastic, and her voice sounded
    exquisitely as she spoke.

My mother looked in delight and amazement at the
    stranger,
She look'd at the freshness of her tall-borne face and
    full and pliant limbs,
The more she look'd upon her she loved her,

Never before had she seen such wonderful beauty and
    purity,
She made her sit on a bench by the jamb of the
    fireplace, she cook'd food for her,
She had no work to give her, but she gave her
    remembrance and fondness.

The red squaw staid all the forenoon, and toward the
    middle of the afternoon she went away,
O my mother was loth to have her go away,
All the week she thought of her, she watch'd for her
    many a month,
She remember'd her many a winter and many a
    summer,
But the red squaw never came nor was heard of there
    again.

7

A show of the summer softness – a contact of
    something unseen – an amour of the light and air,
I am jealous and overwhelm'd with friendliness,
And will go gallivant with the light and air myself.

O love and summer, you are in the dreams and in me,
Autumn and winter are in the dreams, the farmer goes
    with his thrift,
The droves and crops increase, the barns are well-fill'd.
Elements merge in the night, ships make tacks in the
    dreams,
The sailor sails, the exile returns home,
The fugitive returns unharm'd, the immigrant is back
    beyond months and years,
The poor Irishman lives in the simple house of his

childhood with the well-known neighbors and faces,
They warmly welcome him, he is barefoot again, he
forgets he is well off,
The Dutchman voyages home, and the Scotchman and
Welshman voyage home, and the native of the
Mediterranean voyages home,
To every port of England, France, Spain, enter well-
fill'd ships,
The Swiss foots it toward his hills, the Prussian goes
his way, the Hungarian his way, and the Pole his
way,
The Swede returns, and the Dane and Norwegian
return.

The homeward bound and the outward bound,
The beautiful lost swimmer, the ennuyé, the onanist,
the female that loves unrequited, the money-maker,
The actor and actress, those through with their parts
and those waiting to commence,
The affectionate boy, the husband and wife, the voter,
the nominee that is chosen and the nominee that has
fail'd,
The great already known and the great any time after
to-day,
The stammerer, the sick, the perfect-form'd, the
homely,
The criminal that stood in the box, the judge that sat
and sentenced him, the fluent lawyers, the jury, the
audience,
The laughter and weeper, the dancer, the midnight
widow, the red squaw,
The consumptive, the erysipalite, the idiot, he that is
wrong'd,

The antipodes, and every one between this and them in
the dark,
I swear they are averaged now — one is no better than
the other,
The night and sleep have liken'd them and restored
them.

I swear they are all beautiful,
Every one that sleeps is beautiful, every thing in the
dim light is beautiful,
The wildest and bloodiest is over, and all is peace.

Peace is always beautiful,
The myth of heaven indicates peace and night.
The myth of heaven indicates the soul,
The soul is always beautiful, it appears more or it
appears less, it comes or it lags behind,
It comes from its embower'd garden and looks
pleasantly on itself and encloses the world,
Perfect and clean the genitals previously jetting, and
perfect and clean the womb cohering,
The head well-grown proportion'd and plumb, and the
bowels and joints proportion'd and plumb.

The soul is always beautiful,
The universe is duly in order, every thing is in its
place,
What has arrived is in its place and what waits shall be
in its place,
The twisted skull waits, the watery or rotten blood
waits,
The child of the glutton or venerealee waits long, and
the child of the drunkard waits long, and the
drunkard himself waits long,
The sleepers that lived and died wait, the far advanced

are to go on in their turns, and the far behind are
    to come on in their turns,
The diverse shall be no less diverse, but they shall flow
    and unite – they unite now.

8

The sleepers are very beautiful as they lie unclothed,
They flow hand in hand over the whole earth from
    east to west as they lie unclothed,
The Asiatic and African are hand in hand, the European
    and American are hand in hand,
Learn'd and unlearn'd are hand in hand, and male and
    female are hand in hand,
The bare arm of the girl crosses the bare breast of her
    lover, they press close without lust, his lips press her
    neck,
The father holds his grown or ungrown son in his
    arms with measureless love, and the son holds the
    father in his arms with measureless love,
The white hair of the mother shines on the white wrist
    of the daughter,
The breath of the boy goes with the breath of the
    man, friend is inarm'd by friend,
The scholar kisses the teacher and the teacher kisses the
    scholar, the wrong'd is made right,
The call of the slave is one with the master's call, and
    the master salutes the slave,
The felon steps forth from the prison, the insane
    becomes sane, the suffering of sick persons is
    reliev'd.
The sweating and fevers stop, the throat that was
    unsound is sound, the lungs of the consumptive are
    resumed, the poor distress'd head is free,

The joints of the rheumatic move as smoothly as ever,
  and smoother than ever,
Stiflings and passages open, the paralyzed become
  supple,
They swell'd and convuls'd and congested awake to
  themselves in condition,
They pass the invigoration of the night and the
  chemistry of the night, and awake.

I too pass from the night,
I stay a while away O night, but I return to you again
  and love you.

Why should I be afraid to trust myself to you?
I am not afraid, I have been well brought forward by
  you,
I love the rich running day, but I do not desert her in
  whom I lay so long,
I know not how I came of you and I know not where
  I go with you, but I know I came well and shall go
  well.

I will stop only a time with the night, and rise
  betimes,
I will duly pass the day O my mother, and duly return
  to you.

Crossing Brooklyn Ferry

1

Flood-tide below me! I see you face to face!
Clouds of the west – sun there half an hour high – I
    see you also face to face.

Crowds of men and women attired in the usual
    costumes, how curious you are to me!
On the ferry-boats the hundreds and hundreds that
    cross, returning home, are more curious to me than
    you suppose,
And you that shall cross from shore to shore years
    hence are more to me, and more in my meditations,
    than you might suppose.

2

The impalpable sustenance of me from all things at all
    hours of the day,
The simple, compact, well-join'd scheme, myself
    disintegrated, every one disintegrated yet part of the
    scheme,
The similitudes of the past and those of the future,
The glories strung like beads on my smallest sights and
    hearings, on the walk in the street and the passage
    over the river,
The current rushing so swiftly and swimming with me
    far away,
The others that are to follow me, the ties between me
    and them,
The certainty of others, the life, love, sight, hearing of
    others.

Others will enter the gates of the ferry and cross from
  shore to shore,
Others will watch the run of the flood-tide,
Others will see the shipping of Manhattan north and
  west, and the heights of Brooklyn to the south and
  east,
Others will see the islands large and small;
Fifty years hence, others will see them as they cross,
  the sun half an hour high,
A hundred years hence, or ever so many hundred years
  hence, others will see them,
Will enjoy the sunset, the pouring-in of the flood-tide,
  the falling-back to the sea of the ebb-tide.

3

It avails not, time nor place – distance avails not,
I am with you, you men and women of a generation,
  or ever so many generations hence,
Just as you feel when you look on the river and sky,
  so I felt,
Just as any of you is one of a living crowd, I was one
  of a crowd,
Just as you are refresh'd by the gladness of the river
  and the bright flow, I was refresh'd,
Just as you stand and lean on the rail, yet hurry with
  the swift current, I stood yet was hurried,
Just as you look on the numberless masts of ships and
  the thick-stemm'd pipes of steamboats, I look'd.

I too many and many a time cross'd the river of old,
Watched the Twelfth-month sea-gulls, saw them high
  in the air floating with motionless wings, oscillating
  their bodies,

Saw how the glistening yellow lit up parts of their
    bodies and left the rest in strong shadow,
Saw the slow-wheeling circles and the gradual edging
    toward the south,
Saw the reflection of the summer sky in the water,
Had my eyes dazzled by the shimmering track of
    beams,
Look'd at the fine centrifugal spokes of light round the
    shape of my head in the sunlit water,
Look'd on the haze on the hills southward and south-
    westward,
Look'd on the vapor as it flew in fleeces tinged with
    violet,
Look'd toward the lower bay to notice the vessels
    arriving,
Saw their approach, saw aboard those that were near
    me,
Saw the white sails of schooners and sloops, saw the
    ships at anchor,
The sailors at work in the rigging or out astride the
    spars,
The round masts, the swinging motion of the hulls, the
    slender serpentine pennants,
The large and small steamers in motion, the pilots in
    their pilot-houses,
The white wake left by the passage, the quick
    tremulous whirl of the wheels,
The flags of all nations, the falling of them at sunset,
The scallop-edged waves in the twilight, the ladled
    cups, the frolicsome crests and glistening,
The stretch afar growing dimmer and dimmer, the gray
    walls of the granite storehouses by the docks,
On the river the shadowy group, the big steam-tug

closely flank'd on each side by the barges, the hay-
boat, the belated lighter,
On the neighboring shore the fires from the foundry
chimneys burning high and glaringly into the night,
Casting their flicker of black contrasted with wild red
and yellow light over the tops of houses, and down
into the clefts of streets.

4

These and all else were to me the same as they are to
you,
I loved well those cities, loved well the stately and
rapid river,
The men and women I saw were all near to me,
Others the same – others who look back on me
because I look'd forward to them,
(The time will come, though I stop here to-day and
to-night.)

5

What is it then between us?
What is the count of the scores or hundreds of years
between us?

Whatever it is, it avails not – distance avails not, and
place avails not,
I too lived, Brooklyn of ample hills was mine,
I too walk'd the streets of Manhattan island, and bathed
in the waters around it,
I too felt the curious abrupt questionings stir within
me.
In the day among crowds of people sometimes they
came upon me,

In my walks home late at night or as I lay in my bed
    they came upon me,
I too had been struck from the float forever held in
    solution,
I too had receiv'd identity by my body,
That I was I knew was of my body, and what I should
    be I knew I should be of my body.

6

It is not upon you alone the dark patches fall,
The dark threw its patches down upon me also,
The best I had done seem'd to me blank and
    suspicious,
My great thoughts as I supposed them, were they not
    in reality meagre?
Nor is it you alone who know what it is to be evil,
I am he who knew what it was to be evil,

I too knitted the old knot of contrariety,
Blabb'd, blush'd, resented, lied, stole, grudg'd,
Had guile, anger, lust, hot wishes I dared not speak,
Was wayward, vain, greedy, shallow, sly, cowardly,
    malignant,
The wolf, the snake, the hog, not wanting in me,
The cheating look, the frivolous word, the adulterous
    wish, not wanting,
Refusals, hates, postponements, meanness, laziness,
    none of these wanting,
Was one with the rest, the days and haps of the rest,
Was call'd by my nighest name by clear loud voices of
    young men as they saw me approaching or passing,
Felt their arms on my neck as I stood, or the negligent
    leaning of their flesh against me as I sat,
Saw many I loved in the street or ferry-boat or public
    assembly, yet never told them a word,

Lived the same life with the rest, the same old
    laughing, gnawing, sleeping,
Play'd the part that still looks back on the actor or
    actress,
The same old role, the role that is what we make it, as
    great as we like,
Or as small as we like, or both great and small.

7

Closer yet I approach you,
What thought you have of me now, I had as much of
    you — I laid in my stores in advance,
I consider'd long and seriously of you before you were
    born.

Who was to know what should come home to me?
Who knows but I am enjoying this?
Who knows, for all the distance, but I am as good as
    looking at you now, for all you cannot see me?

8

Ah, what can ever be more stately and admirable to
    me than mast-hemm'd Manhattan?
River and sunset and scallop-edg'd waves of flood-tide?
The sea-gulls oscillating their bodies, the hay-boat in
    the twilight, and the belated lighter?
What gods can exceed these that clasp me by the hand,
    and with voices I love call me promptly and loudly
    by my nighest name as I approach?
What is more subtle than this which ties me to the
    woman or man that looks in my face?
Which fuses me into you now, and pours my meaning
    into you?

We understand then do we not?

What I promis'd without mentioning it, have you not accepted?

What the study could not teach — what the preaching could not accomplish is accomplish'd, is it not?

9

Flow on, river! flow with the flood-tide, and ebb with the ebb-tide!

Frolic on, crested and scallop-edg'd waves!

Gorgeous clouds of the sunset! drench with your splendor me, or the men and women generations after me!

Cross from shore to shore, countless crowds of passengers!

Stand up, tall masts of Mannahatta! stand up, beautiful hills of Brooklyn!

Throb, baffled and curious brain! throw out questions and answers!

Suspend here and everywhere, eternal float of solution!

Gaze, loving and thirsting eyes, in the house or street or public assembly!

Sound out, voices of young men! loudly and musically call me by my nighest name!

Live, old life! play the part that looks back on the actor or actress!

Play the old role, the role that is great or small according as one makes it!

Consider, you who peruse me, whether I may not in unknown ways be looking upon you;

Be firm, rail over the river, to support those who lean idly, yet haste with the hasting current;

Fly on, sea-birds! fly sideways, or wheel in large circles
    high in the air;
Receive the summer sky, you water, and faithfully hold
    it till all downcast eyes have time to take it from
    you!
Diverge, fine spokes of light, from the shape of my
    head, or any one's head, in the sunlit water!
Come on, ships from the lower bay! pass up or down,
    white-sail'd schooners, sloops, lighters!
Flaunt away, flags of all nations! be duly lower'd at
    sunset!
Burn high your fires, foundry chimneys! cast black
    shadows at nightfall! cast red and yellow light over
    the tops of the houses!
Appearances, now or henceforth, indicate what you are,
You necessary film, continue to envelop the soul,
About my body for me, and your body for you, be
    hung our divinest aromas,
Thrive, cities – bring your freight, bring your shows,
    ample and sufficient rivers,
Expand, being than which none else is perhaps more
    spiritual,
Keep your places, objects than which none else is more
    lasting,

You have waited, you always wait, you dumb,
    beautiful ministers,
We receive you with free sense at last, and are insatiate
    henceforward,
Not you any more shall be able to foil us, or withhold
    yourselves from us,
We use you, and do not cast you aside – we plant you
    permanently within us,

We fathom you not — we love you — there is
    perfection in you also,
You furnish your parts toward eternity,
Great or small, you furnish your parts toward the soul.

Out of the Cradle Endlessly Rocking

Out of the cradle endlessly rocking,
Out of the mocking-bird's throat, the musical shuttle,
Out of the Ninth-month midnight,
Over the sterile sands and the fields beyond, where the
    child leaving his bed wander'd alone, bareheaded,
    barefoot,
Down from the shower'd halo,
Up from the mystic play of shadows twining and
    twisting as if they were alive,
Out from the patches of briers and blackberries,
From the memories of the bird that chanted to me,
From your memories sad brother, from the fitful
    risings and fallings I heard,
From under that yellow half-moon late-risen and
    swollen as if with tears,
From those beginning notes of yearning and love there
    in the mist,
From the thousand responses of my heart never to
    cease,
From the myriad thence-arous'd words,
From the word stronger and more delicious than any,
From such as now they start the scene revisiting,
As a flock, twittering, rising, or overhead passing,
Borne hither, ere all eludes me, hurriedly,
A man, yet by these tears a little boy again,
Throwing myself on the sand, confronting the waves,
I, chanter of pains and joys, uniter of here and
    hereafter,
Taking all hints to use them, but swiftly leaping
    beyond them,
A reminiscence sing.

Once Paumanok,

When the lilac-scent was in the air and Fifth-month
  grass was growing,

Up this seashore in some briers,

Two feather'd guests from Alabama, two together,

And their nest, and four light-green eggs spotted with
  brown,

And every day the he-bird to and fro near at hand,

And every day the she-bird crouch'd on her nest,
  silent, with bright eyes,

And every day I, a curious boy, never too close, never
  disturbing them,

Cautiously peering, absorbing, translating.

Shine! shine! shine!
Pour down your warmth, great sun!
While we bask, we two together.

Two together!
Winds blow south, or winds blow north,
Day come white, or night come black,
Home, or rivers and mountains from home,
Singing all time, minding no time,
While we two keep together.

Till of a sudden,

May-be kill'd, unknown to her mate,

One forenoon the she-bird crouch'd not on the nest,

Nor return'd that afternoon, nor the next,

Nor ever appear'd again.

And thenceforward all summer in the sound of the sea,

And at night under the full of the moon in calmer
  weather,

Over the hoarse surging of the sea,
Or flitting from brier to brier by day,
I saw, I heard at intervals the remaining one, the he-
    bird,
The solitary guest from Alabama.

Blow! blow! blow!
Blow up sea-winds along Paumanok's shore;
I wait and I wait till you blow my mate to me.

Yes, when the stars glisten'd,
All night long on the prong of a moss-scallop'd stake,
Down almost amid the slapping waves,
Sat the lone singer wonderful causing tears.

He call'd on his mate,
He pour'd forth the meanings which I of all men
    know.

Yes my brother I know,
The rest might not, but I have treasur'd every note,
For more than once dimly down to the beach gliding,
Silent, avoiding the moonbeams, blending myself with
    the shadows,
Recalling now the obscure shapes, the echoes, the
    sounds and sights after their sorts,
The white arms out in the breakers tirelessly tossing,
I, with bare feet, a child, the wind wafting my hair,
Listen'd long and long.

Listen'd to keep, to sing, now translating the notes,
Following you my brother.

Soothe! soothe! soothe!

Close on its wave soothes the wave behind,
And again another behind embracing and lapping, every one close,
But my love soothes not me, not me.

Low hangs the moon, it rose late,
It is lagging — O I think it is heavy with love, with love.

O madly the sea pushes upon the land,
With love, with love.

O night! do I not see my love fluttering out among the breakers?
What is that little black thing I see there in the white?

Loud! loud! loud!
Loud I call to you, my love!
High and clear I shoot my voice over the waves,
Surely you must know who is here, is here,
You must know who I am, my love.

Low-hanging moon!
What is that dusky spot in your brown yellow?
O it is the shape, the shape of my mate!
O moon do not keep her from me any longer.

Land! land! O land!
Whichever way I turn, O I think you could give me my mate back
    again if you only would,
For I am almost sure I see her dimly whichever way I look.

O rising stars!
Perhaps the one I want so much will rise, will rise with some of
    you.
O throat! O trembling throat!
Sound clearer through the atmosphere!

Pierce the woods, the earth,
Somewhere listening to catch you must be the one I want.

Shake out carols!
Solitary here, the night's carols!
Carols of lonesome love! death's carols!
Carols under that lagging, yellow, waning moon!
O under that moon where she droops almost down into the sea!
O reckless despairing carols.

But soft! sink low!
Soft! let me just murmur,
And do you wait a moment you husky-nois'd sea,
For somewhere I believe I heard my mate responding to me,
So faint, I must be still, be still to listen,
But not altogether still, for then she might not come immediately to
    me.

Hither my love!
Here I am! here!
With this just-sustain'd note I announce myself to you,
This gentle call is for you my love, for you.

Do not be decoy'd elsewhere,
That is the whistle of the wind, it is not my voice,
That is the fluttering, the fluttering of the spray,
Those are the shadows of leaves.

O darkness! O in vain!
O I am very sick and sorrowful.

O brown halo in the sky near the moon, drooping upon the sea!
O troubled reflection in the sea!
O throat! O throbbing heart!

And I singing uselessly, uselessly all the night.

O past! O happy life! O songs of joy!
In the air, in the woods, over fields,
Loved! loved! loved! loved! loved!
But my mate no more, no more with me!
We two together no more.

The aria sinking,
All else continuing, the stars shining.
The winds blowing, the notes of the bird continuous
    echoing.
With angry moans the fierce old mother incessantly
    moaning,
On the sands of Paumanok's shore gray and rustling,
The yellow half-moon enlarged, sagging down,
    drooping, the face of the sea almost touching,
The boy ecstatic, with his bare feet the waves, with his
    hair the atmosphere dallying,
The love in the heart long pent, now loose, now at last
    tumultuously bursting,
The aria's meaning, the ears, the soul, swiftly
    depositing,
The strange tears down the cheeks coursing,
The colloquy there, the trio, each uttering,
The undertone, the savage old mother incessantly
    crying,
To the boy's soul's questions sullenly timing, some
    drown'd secret hissing.
To the outsetting bard.

Demon or bird! (said the boy's soul,)
Is it indeed toward your mate you sing? or is it really
    to me?

For I, that was a child, my tongue's use sleeping, now
   I have heard you,
Now in a moment I know what I am for, I awake,
And already a thousand singers, a thousand songs,
   clearer, louder and more sorrowful than yours,
A thousand warbling echoes have started to life within
   me, never to die.

O you singer solitary, singing by yourself, projecting
   me,
O solitary me listening, never more shall I cease
   perpetuating you,
Never more shall I escape, never more the
   reverberations,
Never more the cries of unsatisfied love be absent from
   me,
Never again leave me to be the peaceful child I was
   before what there in the night,
By the sea under the yellow and sagging moon,
The messenger there arous'd, the fire, the sweet hell
   within,
The unknown want, the destiny of me.

O give me the clew! (it lurks in the night here
   somewhere,)
O if I am to have so much, let me have more!

A word then, (for I will conquer it,)
A word final, superior to all,
Subtle, sent-up what is it? — I listen;
Are you whispering it, and have been all the time, you
   sea waves?
Is that it from your liquid rims and wet sands?
Whereto answering, the sea,

Delaying not, hurrying not,
Whisper'd me through the night, and very plainly
     before daybreak,
Lisp'd to me the low and delicious word death,
And again death, death, death, death,
Hissing melodious, neither like the bird nor like my
     arous'd child's heart,
But edging near as privately for me rustling at my feet,
Creeping thence steadily up to my ears and laving me
     softly all over,
Death, death, death, death, death.

Which I do not forget,
But fuse the song of my dusky demon and brother,
That he sang to me in the moonlight on Paumanok's
     gray beach,
With the thousand reponsive songs at random,
My own songs awaked from that hour,
And with them the key, the word up from the waves,
The word of the sweetest song and all songs,
That strong and delicious word which, creeping to my
     feet,
(Or like some old crone rocking the cradle, swathed in
     sweet garments, bending aside,)
The sea whisper'd me.

As I Ebb'd with the Ocean of Life

I

As I ebb'd with the ocean of life,
As I wended the shores I know,
As I walk'd where the ripples continually wash you
  Paumanok,
Where they rustle up hoarse and sibilant,
Where the fierce old mother endlessly cries for her
  castaways,
I musing late in the autumn day, gazing off southward,
Held by this electric self out of the pride of which I
  utter poems,
Was seiz'd by the spirit that trails in the lines
  underfoot,
The rim, the sediment that stands for all the water and
  all the land of the globe.

Fascinated, my eyes reverting from the south, dropt, to
  follow those slender windrows,
Chaff, straw, splinters of wood, weeds, and the sea-
  gluten,
Scum, scales from shining rocks, leaves of salt-lettuce,
  left by the tide,
Miles walking, the sound of breaking waves the other
  side of me,
Paumanok there and then as I thought the old thought
  of likenesses,
These you presented to me you fish-shaped island,
As I wended the shores I know,
As I walk'd with that electric self-seeking types.

2

As I wend to the shores I know not,
As I list to the dirge, the voices of men and women
  wreck'd
As I inhale the impalpable breezes that set in upon me,
As the ocean so mysterious rolls toward me closer and
  closer,
I too but signify at the utmost a little wash'd-up drift,
A few sands and dead leaves to gather,
Gather, and merge myself as part of the sands and
  drift.

O baffled, balk'd, bent to the very earth,
Oppress'd with myself that I have dared to open my
  mouth,
Aware now that amid all that blab whose echoes recoil
  upon me I have not once had the least idea who or
  what I am,
But that before all my arrogant poems the real Me
  stands yet untouch'd, untold, altogether unreach'd,
Withdrawn far, mocking me with mock-congratulatory
  signs and bows,
With peals of distant ironical laughter at every word I
  have written,
Pointing in silence to these songs, and then to the sand
  beneath.
I perceive I have not really understood any thing, not a
  single object, and that no man ever can,
Nature here in sight of the sea taking advantage of me
  to dart upon me and sting me,
Because I have dared to open my mouth to sing at all.

3

You oceans both, I close with you,
We murmur alike reproachfully rolling sands and drift,
  knowing not why,
These little shreds indeed standing for you and me and
  all.
You friable shore with trails of debris,
You fish-shaped island, I take what is underfoot,
What is yours is mine my father.

I too Paumanok,
I too have bubbled up, floated the measureless float,
  and been wash'd on your shores,
I too am but a trail of drift and debris,
I too leave little wrecks upon you, you fish-shaped
  island.

I throw myself upon your breast my father,
I cling to you so that you cannot unloose me,
I hold you so firm till you answer me something.

Kiss me my father,
Touch me with your lips as I touch those I love,
Breathe to me while I hold you close the secret of the
  murmuring I envy.

4

Ebb, ocean of life, (the flow will return,)
Cease not your moaning you fierce old mother,
Endlessly cry for your castaways, but fear not, deny not
  me,
Rustle not up so hoarse and angry against my feet as I
  touch you or gather from you.

I mean tenderly by you and all,
I gather for myself and for this phantom looking down
    where we lead, and following me and mine.

Me and mine, loose windrows, little corpses,
Froth, snowy white, and bubbles,
(See, from my dead lips the ooze exuding at last,
See, the prismatic colors glistening and rolling,)
Tufts of straw, sands, fragments,
Buoy'd hither from many moods, one contradicting
    another,
From the storm, the long calm, the darkness, the swell,
Musing, pondering, a breath, a briny tear, a dab of
    liquid or soil,
Up just as much out of fathomless workings fermented
    and thrown,
A limp blossom or two, torn, just as much over waves
    floating, drifted at random,
Just as much for us that sobbing dirge of Nature,
Just as much whence we come that blare of the cloud-
    trumpets,
We, capricious, brought hither we know not whence,
    spread out before you,
You up there walking or sitting,
Whoever you are, we too lie in drifts at your feet.

I Sing the Body Electric

1

I sing the body electric,
The armies of those I love engirth me and I engirth
 them,
They will not let me off till I go with them, respond
 to them,
And discorrupt them, and charge them full with the
 charge of the soul.

Was it doubted that those who corrupt their own
 bodies conceal themselves?
And if those who defile the living are as bad as they
 who defile the dead?
And if the body does not do fully as much as the soul?
And if the body were not the soul, what is the soul?

2

The love of the body of man or woman balks account,
 the body itself balks account,
That of the male is perfect, and that of the female is
 perfect.

The expression of the face balks account,
But the expression of a well-made man appears not
 only in his face,
It is in his limbs and joints also, it is curiously in the
 joints of his hips and wrists,
It is in his walk, the carriage of his neck, the flex of
 his waist and knees, dress does not hide him,
The strong sweet quality he has strikes through the
 cotton and broadcloth,

To see him pass conveys as much as the best poem, perhaps more,
You linger to see his back, and the back of his neck and shoulder-side.

The sprawl and fulness of babes, the bosoms and heads of women, the folds of their dress, their style as we pass in the street, the contour of their shape downwards,
The swimmer naked in the swimming-bath, seen as he swims through the transparent green-shine, or lies with his face up and rolls silently to and fro in the heave of the water,
The bending forward and backward of rowers in row-boats, the horseman in his saddle,
Girls, mothers, house-keepers, in all their performances,
The group of laborers seated at noon-time with their open dinner-kettles, and their wives waiting,
The female soothing a child, the farmer's daughter in the garden or cow-yard,
The young fellow hoeing corn, the sleigh-driver driving his six horses through the crowd,
The wrestle of wrestlers, two apprentice-boys, quite grown, lusty, good-natured, native-born, out on the vacant lot at sundown after work,
The coats and caps thrown down, the embrace of love and resistance,
The upper-hold and under-hold, the hair rumpled over and blinding the eyes;
The march of firemen in their own costumes, the play of masculine muscle through clean-setting trowsers and waist-straps,
The slow return from the fire, the pause when the bell strikes suddenly again, and the listening on the alert,

The natural, perfect, varied attitudes, the bent head, the
    curv'd neck and the counting;
Such-like I love – I loosen myself, pass freely, am at
    the mother's breast with the little child,
Swim with the swimmers, wrestle with wrestlers,
    march in line with the firemen, and pause, listen,
    count.

3

I knew a man, a common farmer, the father of five
    sons,
And in them the fathers of sons, and in them the
    fathers of sons.

This man was of wonderful vigor, calmness, beauty of
    person,
The shape of his head, the pale yellow and white of
    his hair and beard, the immeasurable meaning of his
    black eyes, the richness and breadth of his manners,
These I used to go and visit him to see, he was wise
    also,
He was six feet tall, he was over eighty years old, his
    sons were massive, clean, bearded, tan-faced,
    handsome,
They and his daughters loved him, all who saw him
    loved him,
They did not love him by allowance, they loved him
    with personal love,
He drank water only, the blood show'd like scarlet
    through the clear-brown skin of his face,
He was a frequent gunner and fisher, he sail'd his boat
    himself, he had a fine one presented to him by a

ship-joiner, he had fowling-pieces presented to him by men that loved him,
When he went with his five sons and many grand-sons to hunt or fish, you would pick him out as the most beautiful and vigorous of the gang,
You would wish long and long to be with him, you would wish to sit by him in the boat that you and he might touch each other.

4

I have perceiv'd that to be with those I like is enough,
To stop in company with the rest at evening is enough,
To be surrounded by beautiful, curious, breathing, laughing flesh is enough,
To pass among them or touch any one, or rest my arm ever so lightly round his or her neck for a moment, what is this then?
I do not ask any more delight, I swim in it as in a sea.

There is something in staying close to men and women and looking on them, and in the contact and odor of them, that pleases the soul well,
All things please the soul, but these please the soul well.

5

This is the female form,
A divine nimbus exhales from it from head to foot,
It attracts with fierce undeniable attraction,
I am drawn by its breath as if I were no more than a helpless vapor, all falls aside but myself and it,
Books, art, religion, time, the visible and solid earth,

and what was expected of heaven or fear'd of hell,
    are now consumed.
Mad filaments, ungovernable shoots play out of it, the
    response likewise ungovernable,
Hair, bosom, hips, bend of legs, negligent falling hands
    all diffused, mine too diffused,
Ebb stung by the flow and flow stung by the ebb,
    love-flesh swelling and deliciously aching,
Limitless limpid jets of love hot and enormous,
    quivering jelly of love, white-blow and delirious
    juice,
Bridegroom night of love working surely and softly
    into the prostrate dawn,
Undulating into the willing and yielding day,
Lost in the cleave of the clasping and sweet-flesh'd day.

This the nucleus – after the child is born of woman,
    man is born of woman,
This the bath of birth, this the merge of small and
    large, and the outlet again.

Be not ashamed women, your privilege encloses the
    rest, and is the exit of the rest,
You are the gates of the body, and you are the gates
    of the soul.

The female contains all qualities and tempers them,
She is in her place and moves with perfect balance,
She is all things duly veil'd, she is both passive and
    active,
She is to conceive daughters as well as sons, and sons
    as well as daughters.

As I see my soul reflected in Nature,

As I see through a mist, One with inexpressible
completeness, sanity, beauty,
See the bent head and arms folded over the breast, the
Female I see.

6

The male is not less the soul nor more, he too is in
his place,
He too is all qualities, he is action and power,
The flush of the known universe is in him,
Scorn becomes him well, and appetite and defiance
become him well,
The wildest largest passions, bliss that is utmost,
sorrow that is utmost become him well, pride is for
him,
The full-spread pride of man is calming and excellent
to the soul,
Knowledge becomes him, he likes it always, he brings
every thing to the test of himself,
Whatever the survey, whatever the sea and the sail he
strikes soundings as last only here,
(Where else does he strike soundings except here?)
The man's body is sacred and the woman's body is
sacred,
No matter who it is, it is sacred — is it the meanest
one in the laborer's gang?
Is it one of the dull-faced immigrants just landed on
the wharf?
Each belongs here or anywhere just as much as the
well-off, just as much as you,
Each has his or her place in the procession.

(All is a procession,

The universe is a procession with measured and perfect
  motion.)

Do you know so much yourself that you call the
  meanest ignorant?
Do you suppose you have a right to a good sight, and
  he or she has no right to a sight?
Do you think matter has cohered together from its
  diffuse float, and the soil is on the surface, and
  water runs and vegetation sprouts,
For you only, and not for him and her?

7

A man's body at auction,
(For before the war I often go to the slave-mart and
  watch the sale,)
I help the auctioneer, the sloven does not half know
  his business.

Gentlemen look on this wonder,
Whatever the bids of the bidders they cannot be high
  enough for it,
For it the globe lay preparing quintillions of years
  without one animal or plant,
For it the revolving cycles truly and steadily roll'd.

In this head the all-baffling brain,
In it and below it the makings of heroes.

Examine these limbs, red, black, or white, they are
  cunning in tendon and nerve,
They shall be stript that you may see them.
Exquisite senses, life-lit eyes, pluck, volition,

Flakes of breast-muscle, pliant backbone and neck, flesh
    not flabby, good-sized arms and legs,
And wonders within there yet.

Within there runs blood,
The same old blood! the same red-running blood!
There swells and jets a heart, there all passions, desires,
    reachings, aspirations,
(Do you think they are not there because they are not
    express'd in parlors and lecture-rooms?)

This is not only one man, this the father of those who
    shall be fathers in their turns,
In him the start of populous states and rich republics,
Of him countless immortal lives with countless
    embodiments and enjoyments.

How do you know who shall come from the offspring
    of his offspring through the centuries?
(Who might you find you have come from yourself, if
    you could trace back through the centuries?)

8

A woman's body at auction,
She too is not only herself, she is the teeming mother
    of mothers,
She is the bearer of them that shall grow and be mates
    to the mothers.

Have you ever loved the body of a woman?
Have you ever loved the body of a man?
Do you not see that these are exactly the same to all in
    all nations and times all over the earth?

If any thing is sacred the human body is sacred,
And the glory and sweat of a man is the token of
　　manhood untainted,
And in man or woman a clean, strong, firm-fibred
　　body, is more beautiful than the most beautiful face.
Have you seen the fool that corrupted his own live
　　body? or the fool that corrupted her own live body?
For they do not conceal themselves, and cannot conceal
　　themselves.

9

O my body! I dare not desert the likes of you in other
　　men and women, nor the likes of the parts of you,
I believe the likes of you are to stand or fall with the
　　likes of the soul (and that they are the soul,)
I believe the likes of you shall stand or fall with my
　　poems, and that they are my poems,
Man's, woman's, child's, youth's, wife's, husband's,
　　mother's, father's, young man's, young woman's
　　poems,
Head, neck, hair, ears, drop and tympan of the ears,
Eyes, eye-fringes, iris of the eye, eyebrows, and the
　　waking or sleeping of the lids,
Mouth, tongue, lips, teeth, roof of the mouth, jaws,
　　and the jaw-hinges,
Nose, nostrils of the nose, and the partition,
Cheeks, temples, forehead, chin, throat, back of the
　　neck, neck-slue,
Strong shoulders, manly beard, scapula, hind-shoulders,
　　and the ample side-round of the chest,
Upper-arm, armpit, elbow-socket, lower-arm, arm-
　　sinews, arm-bones,
Wrist and wrist-joints, hand, palm, knuckles, thumb,
　　fore-finger, finger-joints, finger-nails,

Broad breast-front, curling hair of the breast, breast-bone, breast-side,

Ribs, belly, backbone, joints of the backbone,

Hips, hip-sockets, hip-strength, inward and outward round, man-balls, man-root,

Strong set of thighs, well carrying the trunk above,

Leg-fibres, knee, knee-pan, upper-leg, under-leg,

Ankles, instep, foot-ball, toes, toe-joints, the heel;

All attitudes, all the shapeliness, all the belongings of my or your body or of any one's body, male or female,

The lung-sponges, the stomach-sac, the bowels sweet and clean,

The brain in its folds inside the skull-frame,

Sympathies, heart-valves, palate-valves, sexuality, maternity,

Womanhood and all that is a woman, and the man that comes from woman,

The womb, the teats, nipples, breast-milk, tears, laughter, weeping, love-looks, love-perturbations and risings,

The voice, articulation, language, whispering, shouting aloud,

Food, drink, pulse, digestion, sweat, sleep, walking, swimming,

Poise on the hips, leaping, reclining, embracing, arm-curving and tightening,

The continual changes of the flex of the mouth, and around the eyes,

The skin, the sunburnt shade, freckles, hair,

The curious sympathy one feels when feeling with the hand the naked meat of the body,

The circling rivers the breath, and breathing it in and out,

The beauty of the waist, and thence of the hips, and thence downward toward the knees,
The thin red jellies within you or within me, the bones and the marrow in the bones,
The exquisite realization of health;
O I say these are not the parts and poems of the body only, but of the soul,
O I say now these are the soul!

Spontaneous Me

Spontaneous me, Nature,
The loving day, the mounting sun, the friend I am
    happy with,
The arm of my friend hanging idly over my shoulder,
The hillside whiten'd with blossoms of the mountain
    ash,
The same late in autumn, the hues of red, yellow,
    drab, purple, and light and dark green,
The rich coverlet of the grass, animals and birds, the
    private untrimm'd bank, the primitive apples, the
    pebble-stones,
Beautiful dripping fragments, the negligent list of one
    after another as I happen to call them to me or
    think of them,
The real poems, (what we call poems being merely
    pictures,)
The poems of the privacy of the night, and of men
    like me,
This poem drooping shy and unseen that I always
    carry, and that all men carry.
(Know once for all, avow'd on purpose, wherever are
    men like me, are our lusty lurking masculine
    poems,)
Love-thoughts, love-juice, love-odor, love-yielding,
    love-climbers, and the climbing sap,
Arms and hands of love, lips of love, phallic thumb of
    love, breasts of love, bellies press'd and glued
    together with love,
Earth of chaste love, life that is only life after love,
The body of my love, the body of the woman I love,
    the body of the man, the body of the earth,

Soft forenoon airs that blow from the south-west,

The hairy wild-bee that murmurs and hankers up and down, that gripes the full-grown lady-flower, curves upon her with amorous firm legs, takes his will of her, and holds himself tremulous and tight till he is satisfied;

The wet of woods through the early hours,

Two sleepers at night lying close together as they sleep, one with an arm slanting down across and below the waist of the other,

The smell of apples, aromas from crush'd sage-plant, mint, birch-bark,

The boy's longings, the glow and pressure as he confides to me what he was dreaming,

The dead leaf whirling its spiral whirl and falling still and content to the ground,

The no-form'd stings that sights, people, objects, sting me with,

The hubb'd sting of myself, stinging me as much as it ever can any one,

The sensitive, orbic, underlapp'd brothers, that only privileged feelers may be intimate where they are,

The curious roamer the hand roaming all over the body, the bashful withdrawing of flesh where the fingers soothingly pause and edge themselves,

The limpid liquid within the young man,

The vex'd corrosion so pensive and so painful,

The torment, the irritable tide that will not be at rest,

The like of the same I feel, the like of the same in others,

The young man that flushes and flushes, and the young woman that flushes and flushes,

The young man that wakes deep at night, the hot hand seeking to repress what would master him,

The mystic amorous night, the strange half-welcome
pangs, visions, sweats,
The pulse pounding through palms and trembling
encircling fingers, the young man all color'd, red,
ashamed, angry;
The souse upon me of my lover the sea, as I lie
willing and naked,
The merriment of the twin babes that crawl over the
grass in the sun, the mother never turning her
vigilant eyes from them,
The walnut-trunk, the walnut-husks, and the ripening
or ripen'd long-round walnuts,
The continence of vegetables, birds, animals,
The consequent meanness of me should I skulk or find
myself indecent, while birds and animals never once
skulk or find themselves indecent,
The great chastity of paternity, to match the great
chastity of maternity,
The oath of procreation I have sworn, my Adamic and
fresh daughters,
The greed that eats me day and night with hungry
gnaw, till I saturate what shall produce boys to fill
my place when I am through,
The wholesome relief, repose, content,
And this bunch pluck'd at random from myself,
It has done its work — I toss it carelessly to fall where
it may.

As Adam Early in the Morning

As Adam early in the morning,
Walking forth from the bower refresh'd with sleep,
Behold me where I pass, hear my voice, approach,
Touch me, touch the palm of your hand to my body
    as I pass,
Be not afraid of my body.

In Paths Untrodden

In paths untrodden,
In the growths by margins of pond-waters,
Escaped from the life that exhibits itself,
From all the standards hitherto publish'd, from the
    pleasures, profits, conformities,
Which too long I was offering to feed my soul,
Clear to me now standards not yet publish'd, clear to
    me that my soul,
That the soul of the man I speak for rejoices in
    comrades,
Here by myself away from the clank of the world,
Tallying and talk'd to here by tongues aromatic,
No longer abash'd (for in this secluded spot I can
    respond as I would not dare elsewhere,)
Strong upon me the life that does not exhibit itself, yet
    contains all the rest,
Resolv'd to sing no songs to-day but those of manly
    attachment,
Projecting them along that substantial life,
Bequeathing hence types of athletic love,
Afternoon this delicious Ninth-month in my forty-first
    year,
I proceed for all who are or have been young men,
To tell the secret of my nights and days,
To celebrate the need of comrades.

We Two, How Long We Were Fool'd

We two, how long we were fool'd,
Now transmuted, we swiftly escape as Nature escapes,
We are Nature, long have we been absent, but now we
    return,
We become plants, trunks, foliage, roots, bark,
We are bedded in the ground, we are rocks,
We are oaks, we grow in the openings side by side,
We browse, we are two among the wild herds
    spontaneous as any,
We are two fishes swimming in the sea together,
We are what locust blossoms are, we drop scent
    around lanes mornings and evenings,
We are also the coarse smut of beasts, vegetables,
    minerals,
We are two predatory hawks, we soar above and look
    down,
We are two resplendent suns, we it is who balance
    ourselves orbic and stellar, we are as two comets,
We prowl fang'd and four-footed in the woods, we
    spring on prey,
We are two clouds forenoons and afternoons driving
    overhead,
We are seas mingling, we are two of those cheerful
    waves rolling over each other and interwetting each
    other,
We are what the atmosphere is, transparent, receptive,
    pervious, impervious,
We are snow, rain, cold, darkness, we are each product
    and influence of the globe,
We have circled and circled till we have arrived home
    again, we two,

We have voided all but freedom and all but our own
  joy.

Native Moments

Native moments – when you come upon me – ah you
  are here now,
Give me now libidinous joys only,
Give me the drench of my passions, give me life coarse
  and rank,
To-day I go consort with Nature's darlings, to-night
  too,
I am for those who believe in loose delights, I share
  the mid-night orgies of young men,
I dance with the dancers and drink with the drinkers,
The echoes ring with our indecent calls, I pick out
  some low person for my dearest friend,
He shall be lawless, rude, illiterate, he shall be one
  condemned by others for deeds done,
I will play a part no longer, why should I exile myself
  from my companions?
O you shunn'd persons, I at least do not shun you,
I come forthwith in your midst, I will be your poet,
I will be more to you than to any of the rest.

These I Singing in Spring

These I singing in spring collect for lovers,
(For who but I should understand lovers and all their
    sorrow and joy?
And who but I should be the poet of comrades?)
Collecting I traverse the garden the world, but soon I
    pass the gates,
Now along the pond-side, now wading in a little,
    fearing not the wet,
Now by the post-and-rail fences where the old stones
    thrown there, pick'd from the fields, have
    accumulated,
(Wild-flowers and vines and weeds come up through
    the stones and partly cover them, beyond these I
    pass,)
For, far in the forest, or sauntering later in summer,
    before I think where I go,
Solitary, smelling the earthy smell, stopping now and
    then in the silence,
Alone I had thought, yet soon a troop gathers around
    me,
Some walk by my side and some behind, and some
    embrace my arms or neck,
They the spirits of dear friends dead or alive, thicker
    they come, a great crowd, and I in the middle,
Collecting, dispensing, singing, there I wander with
    them,
Plucking something for tokens, tossing toward whoever
    is near me,
Here, lilac, with a branch of pine,
Here, out of my pocket, some moss which I pull'd off
    a live-oak in Florida as it hung trailing down,

Here, some pinks and laurel leaves, and a handful of
  sage,
And here what I now draw from the water, wading in
  the pond-side,
(O here I last saw him that tenderly loves me, and
  returns again never to separate from me,
And this, O this shall henceforth be the token of
  comrades, this calamus-root shall,
Interchange it youths with each other! let none render
  it back!)
And twigs of maple and a bunch of wild orange and
  chestnut,
And stems of currants and plum-blows, and the
  aromatic cedar,
These I compass'd around by a thick cloud of spirits,
Wandering, point to or touch as I pass, or throw them
  loosely from me,
Indicating to each one what he shall have, giving
  something to each;
But what I drew from the water by the pond-side, that
  I reserve,
I will give it, but only to them that love as I myself
  am capable of loving.

A Glimpse

A glimpse through an interstice caught,
Of a crowd of workmen and drivers in a bar-room
    around the stove late of a winter night, and I
    unremark'd seated in a corner,
Of a youth who loves me and whom I love, silently
    approaching and seating himself near, that he may
    hold me by the hand,
A long while amid the noises of coming and going, of
    drinking and oath and smutty jest,
There we two, content, happy in being together,
    speaking little, perhaps not a word.

I Saw in Louisiana a Live-Oak Growing

I saw in Louisiana a live-oak growing,
All alone stood it and the moss hung down from the
branches,
Without any companion it grew there uttering joyous
leaves of dark green,
And its look, rude, unbending, lusty, made me think of
myself,
But I wonder'd how it could utter joyous leaves
standing alone there without its friend near, for I
knew I could not,
And I broke off a twig with a certain number of leaves
upon it, and twined around it a little moss,
And brought it away, and I have placed it in sight, in
my room,
It is not needed to remind me as of my own dear
friends,
(For I believe lately I think of little else than of them,)
Yet it remains to me a curious token, it makes me
think of manly love;
For all that, and though the live-oak glistens there in
Louisiana solitary in a wide flat space,
Uttering joyous leaves all its life without a friend a
lover near,
I know very well I could not.

Scented Herbage of My Breast

Scented herbage of my breast,
Leaves from you I glean, I write, to be perused best
  afterwards,
Tomb-leaves, body-leaves growing up above me above
  death,
Perennial roots, tall leaves, O the winter shall not
  freeze you delicate leaves,
Every year shall you bloom again, out from where you
  retired you shall emerge again;
O I do not know whether many passing by will
  discover you or inhale your faint odor, but I believe
  a few will;
O slender leaves! O blossoms of my blood! I permit
  you to tell in your own way of the heart that is
  under you,
O I do not know what you mean there underneath
  yourselves, you are not happiness,
You are often more bitter than I can bear, you burn
  and sting me,
Yet you are beautiful to me you faint tinged roots, you
  make me think of death,
Death is beautiful from you, (what indeed is finally
  beautiful except death and love?)
O I think it is not for life I am chanting here my chant
  of lovers, I think it must be for death,
For how calm, how solemn it grows to ascend to the
  atmosphere of lovers,
Death or life I am then indifferent, my soul declines to
  prefer,
(I am not sure but the high soul of lovers welcomes
  death most,)

Indeed O death, I think now these leaves mean
   precisely the same as you mean,
Grow up taller sweet leaves that I may see! grow up
   out of my breast!
Spring away from the conceal'd heart there!
Do not fold yourself so in your pink-tinged roots timid
   leaves!
Do not remain down there so ashamed, herbage of my
   breast!
Come I am determin'd to unbare this broad breast of
   mine, I have long enough stifled and choked;
Emblematic and capricious blades I leave you, now you
   serve me not,
I will say what I have to say by itself,
I will sound myself and comrades only, I will never
   again utter a call only their call,
I will raise with it immortal reverberations through the
   States,
I will give an example to lovers to take permanent
   shape and will through the States,
Through me shall the words be said to make death
   exhilarating,
Give me your tone therefore O death, that I may
   accord with it,
Give me yourself, for I see that you belong to me now
   above all, and are folded inseparably together, you
   love and death are,
Nor will I allow you to balk me any more with what I
   was calling life,
For now it is convey'd to me that you are the purports
   essential,
That you hide in these shifting forms of life, for
   reasons, and that they are mainly for you,

That you beyond them come forth to remain, the real
    reality,
That behind the mask of materials you patiently wait,
    no matter how long,
That you will one day perhaps take control of all,
That you will perhaps dissipate this entire show of
    appearance,
That may-be you are what it is all for, but it does not
    last so very long,
But you will last very long.

Of the Terrible Doubt of Appearances

Of the terrible doubt of appearances,
Of the uncertainty after all, that we may be deluded,
That may-be reliance and hope are but speculations
    after all,
That may-be identity beyond the grave is a beautiful
    fable only,
May-be the things I perceive, the animals, plants, men,
    hills, shining and flowing waters,
The skies of day and night, colors, densities, forms,
    may-be these are (as doubtless they are) only
    apparitions, and the real something has yet to be
    known,
(How often they dart out of themselves as if to
    confound me and mock me!
How often I think neither I know, nor any man
    knows, aught of them,)
May-be seeming to me what they are (as doubtless
    they indeed but seem) as from my present point of
    view, and might prove (as of course they would)
    nought of what they appear, or nought anyhow,
    from entirely changed points of view;
To me these and the like of these are curiously
    answer'd by my lovers, my dear friends,
When he whom I love travels with me or sits a long
    while holding me by the hand,
When the subtle air, the impalpable, the sense that
    words and reason hold not, surround us and pervade
    us,
Then I am charged with untold and untellable wisdom,
    I am silent, I require nothing further,

I cannot answer the question of appearances or that of
    identity beyond the grave,
But I walk or sit indifferent, I am satisfied,
He ahold of my hand has completely satisfied me.

A March in the Ranks Hard-Prest, and the Road Unknown

A march in the ranks hard-prest, and the road
   unknown,
A route through a heavy wood with muffled steps in
   the darkness,
Our army foil'd with loss severe, and the sullen
   remnant retreating,
Till after midnight glimmer upon us the lights of a
   dim-lighted building,
We come to an open space in the woods, and halt by
   the dim-lighted building,
'Tis a large old church at the crossing roads, now an
   impromptu hospital,
Entering but for a minute I see a sight beyond all the
   pictures and poems ever made,
Shadows of deepest, deepest black, just lit by moving
   candles and lamps,
And by one great pitchy torch stationary with wild red
   flame and clouds of smoke,
By these, crowds, groups of forms vaguely I see on the
   floor, some in the pews laid down,
At my feet more distinctly a soldier, a mere lad, in
   danger of bleeding to death, (he is shot in the
   abdomen,)
I staunch the blood temporarily, (the youngster's face
   is white as a lily,)
Then before I depart I sweep my eyes o'er the scene
   fain to absorb it all,
Faces, varieties, postures beyond description, most in
   obscurity, some of them dead,

Surgeons operating, attendants holding lights, the smell
of ether, the odor of blood,

The crowd, O the crowd of the bloody forms, the yard
outside also fill'd,

Some on the bare ground, some on planks or
stretchers, some in the death-spasm sweating,

An occasional scream or cry, the doctor's shouted
orders or calls,

The glisten of the little steel instruments catching the
glint of the torches,

These I resume as I chant, I see again the forms, I
smell the odor,

Then hear outside the orders given, *Fall in, my men, fall
in;*

But first I bend to the dying lad, his eyes open, a half-
smile gives he me,

Then the eyes close, calmly close, and I speed forth to
the darkness,

Resuming, marching, ever in darkness marching, on in
the ranks,

The unknown road still marching.

The Wound-Dresser

1

An old man bending I come among new faces,
Years looking backward resuming in answer to
    children,
Come tell us old man, as from young men and
    maidens that love me,
(Arous'd and angry, I'd thought to beat the alarum,
    and urge relentless war,
But soon my fingers fail'd me, my face droop'd and I
    resign'd myself,
To sit by the wounded and soothe them, or silently
    watch the dead;)
Years hence of these scenes, of these furious passions,
    these chances,
Of unsurpass'd heroes, (was one side so brave? the
    other was equally brave;)
Now be witness again, paint the mightiest armies of
    earth,
Of those armies so rapid so wondrous what saw you to
    tell us?
What stays with you latest and deepest? of curious
    panics,
Of hard-fought engagements or sieges tremendous what
    deepest remains?

2

O maidens and young men I love and that love me,
What you ask of my days those the strangest and
    sudden your talking recalls,
Soldier alert I arrive after a long march cover'd with
    sweat and dust,

In the nick of time I come, plunge in the fight, loudly
    shout in the rush of successful charge,
Enter the captur'd works – yet lo, like a swift running
    river they fade,
Pass and are gone they fade – I dwell not on soldiers'
    perils or soldiers' joys,
(Both I remember well – many of the hardships, few
    the joys, yet I was content.)

But in silence, in dreams' projections,
While the world of gain and appearance and mirth
    goes on,
So soon what is over forgotten, and waves wash the
    imprints off the sand,
With hinged knees returning I enter the doors, (while
    for you up there,
Whoever you are, follow without noise and be of
    strong heart.)

Bearing the bandages, water and sponge,
Straight and swift to my wounded I go,
Where they lie on the ground after the battle brought
    in,
Where their priceless blood reddens the grass the
    ground,
Or to the rows of the hospital tent, or under the
    roof'd hospital,
To the long rows of cots up and down each side I
    return,
To each and all one after another I draw near, not one
    do I miss,
An attendant follows holding a tray, he carries a refuse
    pail,

Soon to be fill'd with clotted rags and blood, emptied,
    and fill'd again.

I onward go, I stop,
With hinged knees and steady hand to dress wounds,
I am firm with each, the pangs are sharp yet
    unavoidable,
One turns to me his appealing eyes – poor boy! I
    never knew you,
Yet I think I could not refuse this moment to die for
    you, if that would save you.

3

On, on I go, (open doors of time! open hospital
    doors!)
The crush'd head I dress, (poor crazed hand tear not
    the bandage away,)
The neck of the cavalry-man with the bullet through
    and through I examine,
Hard the breathing rattles, quite glazed already the eye,
    yet life struggles hard,
(Come sweet death! be persuaded O beautiful death!
In mercy come quickly.)

From the stump of the arm, the amputated hand,
I undo the clotted lint, remove the slough, wash off
    the matter and blood,
Back on his pillow the soldier bends with curv'd neck
    and side falling head,
His eyes are closed, his face is pale, he dares not look
    on the bloody stump,
And has not yet look'd on it.

I dress a wound in the side, deep, deep,
But a day or two more, for see the frame all wasted
    and sinking,
And the yellow-blue countenance see.

I dress the perforated shoulder, the foot with the
    bullet-wound,
Cleanse the one with a gnawing and putrid gangrene,
    so sickening, so offensive,
While the attendant stands behind aside me holding the
    tray and pail.

I am faithful, I do not give out,
The fractur'd thigh, the knee, the wound in the
    abdomen,
These and more I dress with impassive hand, (yet deep
    in my breast a fire, a burning flame.)

4

Thus in silence in dreams' projections,
Returning, resuming, I thread my way through the
    hospitals,
The hurt and wounded I pacify with soothing hand,
I sit by the restless all the dark night, some are so
    young,
Some suffer so much, I recall the experience sweet and
    sad,
(Many a soldier's loving arms about this neck have
    cross'd and rested,
Many a soldier's kiss dwells on these bearded lips.)

Reconciliation

Word over all, beautiful as the sky,
Beautiful that war and all its deeds of carnage must in
　　time be utterly lost,
That the hands of the sisters Death and Night
　　incessantly softly wash again, and ever again, this
　　soil'd world;
For my enemy is dead, a man divine as myself is dead,
I look where he lies white-faced and still in the coffin
　　— I draw near,
Bend down and touch lightly with my lips the white
　　face in the coffin.

When Lilacs Last in the Dooryard Bloom'd

1

When lilacs last in the dooryard bloom'd,
And the great star early droop'd in the western sky in
the night,
I mourn'd, and yet shall mourn with ever-returning
spring.

Ever-returning spring, trinity sure to me you bring,
Lilac blooming perennial and drooping star in the west,
And thought of him I love.

2

O powerful western fallen star!
O shades of night – O moody, tearful night!
O great star disappear'd – O the black murk that hides
the star!
O cruel hands that hold me powerless – O helpless
soul of me!
O harsh surrounding cloud that will not free my soul.

3

In the dooryard fronting an old farm-house near the
white-wash'd palings,
Stands the lilac-bush tall-growing with heart-shaped
leaves of rich green,
With many a pointed blossom rising delicate, with the
perfume strong I love,
With every leaf a miracle – and from this bush in the
dooryard,

With delicate-color'd blossoms and heart-shaped leaves
   of rich green,
A sprig with its flower I break.

4

In the swamp in secluded recesses,
A shy and hidden bird is warbling a song.

Solitary the thrush,
The hermit withdrawn to himself, avoiding the
   settlements,
Sings by himself a song.

Song of the bleeding throat,
Death's outlet song of life, (for well dear brother I
   knew,
If thou wast not granted to sing thou would'st surely
   die.)

5

Over the breast of the spring, the land, amid cities,
Amid lanes and through old woods, where lately the
   violets peep'd from the ground, spotting the gray
   debris,
Amid the grass in the fields each side of the lanes,
   passing the endless grass,
Passing the yellow-spear'd wheat, every grain from its
   shroud in the dark-brown fields uprisen,
Passing the apple-tree blows of white and pink in the
   orchards,
Carrying a corpse to where it shall rest in the grave,
Night and day journeys a coffin.

6

Coffin that passes through lanes and streets,
Through day and night with the great cloud darkening
  the land,
With the pomp of the inloop'd flags with the cities
  draped in black,
With the show of the States themselves as of crape-
  veil'd women standing,
With processions long and winding and the flambeaus
  of the night,
With the countless torches lit, with the silent sea of
  faces and the unbared heads,
With the waiting depot, the arriving coffin, and the
  somber faces,
With dirges through the night, with the thousand
  voices rising strong and solemn,
With all the mournful voices of the dirges pour'd
  around the coffin,
The dim-lit churches and the shuddering organs —
  where amid these you journey,
With the tolling tolling bells' perpetual clang,
Here, coffin that slowly passes,
I give you my sprig of lilac.

7

(Nor for you, for one alone,
Blossoms and branches green to coffins all I bring,
For fresh as the morning, thus would I chant a song
  for you
          O sane and sacred death.

All over bouquets of roses,
O death, I cover you over with roses and early lilies,

But mostly and now the lilac that blooms the first,
Copious I break, I break the sprigs from the bushes,
With loaded arms I come, pouring for you,
For you and the coffins all of you O death.)

8

O western orb sailing the heaven,
Now I know what you must have meant as a month
    since I walk'd,
As I walk'd in silence the transparent shadowy night,
As I saw you had something to tell as you bent to me
    night after night,
As you droop'd from the sky low down as if to my
    side, (while the other stars all look'd on,)
As we wander'd together the solemn night, (for
    something I know not what kept me from sleep,)
As the night advanced, and I saw on the rim of the
    west how full you were of woe,
As I stood on the rising ground in the breeze in the
    cool transparent night,
As I watch'd where you pass'd and was lost in the
    netherward black of the night,
As my soul in its trouble dissatisfied sank, as where
    you sad orb,
Concluded, dropt in the night, and was gone.

9

Sing on there in the swamp,
O singer bashful and tender, I hear your notes, I hear
    your call,
I hear, I come presently, I understand you,
But a moment I linger, for the lustrous star has
    detain'd me,

The star my departing comrade holds and detains me.

10

O how shall I warble myself for the dead one there I
  loved?
And how shall I deck my song for the large sweet soul
  that has gone?
And what shall my perfume be for the grave of him I
  love?

Sea-winds blown from east and west,
Blown from the Eastern sea and blown from the
  Western sea, till there on the prairies meeting,
These and with these and the breath of my chant,
I'll perfume the grave of him I love.

11

O what shall I hang on the chamber walls?
And what shall the pictures be that I hang on the
  walls,
To adorn the burial-house of him I love?

Pictures of growing spring and farms and homes,
With the Fourth-month eve at sundown, and the gray
  smoke lucid and bright,
With floods of the yellow gold of the gorgeous,
  indolent, sinking sun, burning, expanding the air,
With the fresh sweet herbage under foot, and the pale
  green leaves of the trees prolific,
In the distance the flowing glaze, the breast of the
  river, with a wind-dapple here and there,
With ranging hills on the banks, with many a line
  against the sky, and shadows,

And the city at hand with dwellings so dense, and
    stacks of chimneys,
And all the scenes of life and the workshops, and the
    workmen homeward returning.

12

Lo, body and soul – this land,
My own Manhattan with spires, and the sparkling and
    hurrying tides, and the ships,
The varied and ample land, the South and the North in
    the light, Ohio's shores and flashing Missouri,
And ever the far-spreading prairies cover'd with grass
    and corn.

Lo, the most excellent sun so calm and haughty,
The violet and purple morn with just-felt breezes,
The gentle soft-born measureless light,
The miracle spreading bathing all, the fulfill'd noon,
The coming eve delicious, the welcome night and the
    stars,
Over my cities shining all, enveloping man and land.

13

Sing on, sing on you gray-brown bird,
Sing from the swamps, the recesses, pour your chant
    from the bushes,
Limitless out of the dusk, out of the cedars and pines.

Sing on dearest brother, warble your reedy song,
Loud human song, with voice of uttermost woe.

O liquid and free and tender!
O wild and loose to my soul – O wondrous singer!

You only I hear — yet the star holds me, (but will soon
    depart,)
Yet the lilac with mastering odor holds me.

14

Now while I sat in the day and look'd forth,
In the close of the day with its light and the fields of
    spring, and the farmers preparing their crops,
In the large unconscious scenery of my land with its
    lakes and forests,
In the heavenly aerial beauty, (after the perturb'd
    winds and the storms,)
Under the arching heavens of the afternoon swift
    passing, and the voices of children and women,
The many-moving sea-tides, and I saw the ships how
    they sail'd,
And the summer approaching with richness, and the
    fields all busy with labor,
And the infinite separate houses, how they all went on,
    each with its meals and minutia of daily usages,
And the streets how their throbbings throbb'd, and the
    cities pent — lo, then and there,
Falling upon them all and among them all, enveloping
    me with the rest,
Appear'd the cloud, appear'd the long black trail,
And I knew death, its thought, and the sacred
    knowledge of death.

Then with the knowledge of death as walking one side
    of me,
And the thought of death close-walking the other side
    of me,
And I in the middle as with companions, and as

holding the hands of companions,
I fled forth to the hiding receiving night that talks not,
Down to the shores of the water, the path by the
swamp in the dimness,
To the solemn shadowy cedars and ghostly pines so
still.

And the singer so shy to the rest receiv'd me,
The gray-brown bird I know receiv'd us comrades
three,
And he sang the carol of death, and a verse for him I
love.

From deep secluded recesses,
From the fragrant cedars and the ghostly pines so still,
Came the carol of the bird.

And the charm of the carol rapt me,
As I held as if by their hands my comrades in the
night,
And the voice of my spirit tallied the song of the bird.

Come lovely and soothing death,
Undulate round the world, serenely arriving, arriving,
In the day, in the night, to all, to each,
Sooner or later delicate death.

Prais'd be the fathomless universe,
For life and joy, and for objects and knowledge curious,
And for love, sweet love — but praise! praise! praise!
For the sure-enwinding arms of cool-enfolding death.

Dark mother always gliding near with soft feet,
Have none chanted for thee a chant of fullest welcome?

Then I chant it for thee, I glorify thee above all,
I bring thee a song that when thou must indeed come, come
    unfalteringly.

Approach strong deliveress,
When it is so, when thou hast taken them I joyously sing the dead,
Lost in the loving floating ocean of thee,
Laved in the flood of thy bliss O death.

From me to thee glad serenades,
Dances for thee I propose saluting thee, adornments and feastings for
    thee,
And the sights of the open landscape and the high-spread sky are
    fitting,
And life and the fields, and the huge and thoughtful night.

The night in silence under many a star,
The ocean shore and the husky whispering wave whose voice I know,
And the soul turning to thee O vast and well-veil'd death,
And the body gratefully nestling close to thee.

Over the tree-tops I float thee a song,
Over the rising and sinking waves, over the myriad fields and the
    prairies wide,
Over the dense-pack'd cities all and the teeming wharves and ways,
I float this carol with joy, with joy to thee O death.

15

To the tally of my soul,
Loud and strong kept up the gray-brown bird,
With pure deliberate notes spreading filling the night.

Loud in the pines and cedars dim,

Clear in the freshness moist and the swamp-perfume,
And I with my comrades there in the night.

While my sight that was bound in my eyes unclosed,
As to long panoramas of visions.

And I saw askant the armies,
I saw as in noiseless dreams hundreds of battle-flags,
Borne through the smoke of the battles and pierc'd
    with missiles I saw them,
And carried hither and yon through the smoke, and
    torn and bloody,
And at last but a few shreds left on the staffs, (and all
    in silence,)
And the staffs all splinter'd and broken.

I saw battle-corpses, myriads of them,
And the white skeletons of young men, I saw them,
I saw the debris and debris of all the slain soldiers of
    the war,
But I saw they were not as was thought,
They themselves were fully at rest, they suffer'd not,
The living remain'd and suffer'd, the mother suffer'd,
And the wife and the child and the musing comrade
    suffer'd,
And the armies that remain'd suffer'd.

16

Passing the visions, passing the night,
Passing, unloosing the hold of my comrades' hands,
Passing the song of the hermit bird and the tallying
    song of my soul,
Victorious song, death's outlet song, yet varying ever-

altering song,
As low and wailing, yet clear the notes, rising and
falling, flooding the night,
Sadly sinking and fainting, as warning and warning,
and yet again bursting with joy,
Covering the earth and filling the spread of the heaven,
As that powerful psalm in the night I heard from
recesses,
Passing, I leave thee lilac with heart-shaped leaves,
I leave thee there in the dooryard, blooming,
returning with spring.

I cease from my song for thee,
From my gaze on thee in the west, fronting the west,
communing with thee,
O comrade lustrous with silver face in the night.

Yet each to keep and all, retrievements out of the
night,
The song, the wondrous chant of the gray-brown bird,
And the tallying chant, the echo arous'd in my soul,
With the lustrous and drooping star with the
countenance full of woe,
With the holders holding my hand nearing the call of
the bird,
Comrades mine and I in the midst, and their memory
ever to keep, for the dead I loved so well,
For the sweetest, wisest soul of all my days and lands
— and this for his dear sake,
Lilac and star and bird twined with the chant of my
soul,
There in the fragrant pines and the cedars dusk and
dim.

When I Heard the Learn'd Astronomer

When I heard the learn'd astronomer,
When the proofs, the figures, were ranged in columns
    before me,
When I was shown the charts and diagrams, to add,
    divide, and measure them,
When I sitting heard the astronomer where he lectured
    with much applause in the lecture-room,
How soon unaccountable I became tired and sick,
Till rising and gliding out I wander'd off by myself,
In the mystical moist night-air, and from time to time,
Look'd up in perfect silence at the stars.

A Noiseless Patient Spider

A noiseless patient spider,
I mark'd where on a little promontory it stood isolated,
Mark'd how to explore the vacant vast surrounding,
It launched forth, filament, filament, filament, out of
    itself,
Ever unreeling them, ever tirelessly speeding them.

And you O my soul where you stand,
Surrounded, detached, in measureless oceans of space,
Ceaselessly musing, venturing, throwing, seeking the
    spheres to connect them,
Till the bridge you will need be form'd, till the ductile
    anchor hold,
Till the gossamer thread you fling catch somewhere, O
    my soul.

Sparkles from the Wheel

Where the city's ceaseless crowd moves on the livelong
    day,
Withdrawn I join a group of children watching, I
    pause aside with them.

By the curb toward the edge of the flagging,
A knife-grinder works at his wheel sharpening a great
    knife,
Bending over he carefully holds it to the stone, by foot
    and knee,
With measur'd tread he turns rapidly, as he presses
    with light but firm hand,
Forth issue then in copious golden jets,
Sparkles from the wheel.

The scene and all its belongings, how they seize and
    affect me,
The sad sharp-chinn'd old man with worn clothes and
    broad shoulder-band of leather,
Myself effusing and fluid, a phantom curiously floating,
    now here absorb'd and arrested,
The group, (an unminded point set in a vast
    surrounding,)
The attentive, quiet children, the loud, proud, restive
    base of the streets,
The low hoarse purr of the whirling stone, the light-
    press'd blade,
Diffusing, dropping, sideways-darting, in tiny showers
    of gold,
Sparkles from the wheel.

The Dalliance of the Eagles

Skirting the river road, (my forenoon walk, my rest,)
Skyward in air a sudden muffled sound, the dalliance
of the eagles,
The rushing amorous contact high in space together,
The clinching interlocking claws, a living, fierce,
gyrating wheel,
Four beating wings, two beaks, a swirling mass tight
grappling,
In tumbling turning clustering loops, straight
downward falling,
Till o'er the river pois'd, the twain yet one, a
moment's lull,
A motionless still balance in the air, then parting,
talons loosing,
Upward again on slow-firm pinions slanting, their
separate diverse flight,
She hers, he his, pursuing.

A Clear Midnight

This is thy hour O Soul, thy free flight into the
    wordless,
Away from books, away from art, the day erased, the
    lesson done,
Thee fully forth emerging, silent, gazing, pondering the
    themes thou lovest best,
Night, sleep, death and the stars.

Chronology of Whitman's Life

Year	Age	Life
1819		Born 31 May, on Long Island; second child of Walter Whitman, house builder, and Louisa Van Velsor
1823	3	Whitman family moves to Brooklyn
1825–30	6–11	Whitman attends public school in Brooklyn
1831–5	12–16	Learns printing trade
1836–8	16–19	School teaching, later resumed at intervals.
1838–9	19–20	Publishes and edits the weekly *Long-Islander*; writes poetry and prose
1841	22	Moves to New York City; printing work, Democratic party politics. Publishes stories
1842–7	23–8	Various jobs as journalist and editor. Publishes *Franklin Evans* (1842), a temperance novel.
1848	29	Three months in New Orleans as editor of the *Crescent*
1848–9	29–30	Edits *Brooklyn Freeman*
1850–4	31–5	Freelance journalism, topical poems. House building. Runs printing office and stationery store
1855	36	First (anonymous) edition of *Leaves of Grass*. Father dies

Chronology of his Times

Year	Literary Context	Historical Events
1819		Purchase of Florida from Spain
1823		Proclamation of the Monroe Doctrine
1829		Andrew Jackson elected President of the US
1836	Emerson, *Nature*	
1839	Poe, *Tales of the Grotesque and Arabesque*	
1841	Emerson, *Essays* (first series)	
1842	Tennyson, *Poems*	
1844	Emerson, *Essays* (second series)	
1849		California Gold Rush Fugitive Slave Law
1850	Hawthorne, *The Scarlet Letter*; Tennyson, *In Memoriam*	
1851	Melville, *Moby-Dick*	
1854	Thoreau, *Walden*	Republican Party re-formed on an anti-slavery basis
1855	Longfellow, *The Song of Hiawatha*	

Year	Age	Life
1856		Second edition of *Leaves of Grass*
1857–9	37–40	Edits *Brooklyn Times*
1860	40	Third edition of *Leaves of Grass*, published in Boston
1862–4	43–4	Visits brother wounded at Fredericksburg and remains in Washington DC, visiting soldiers
1865	45	*Drum-Taps* and *Sequel to Drum-Taps*
1867	48	Fourth edition of *Leaves of Grass*
1868	49	William Rossetti's expurgated selection, *Poems of Walt Whitman*, published in England
1871	50–51	Fifth edition of *Leaves of Grass*. *Democratic Vistas*.
1873	53–4	Paralytic stroke. Mother dies. Goes to live with brother George in Camden, New Jersey
1875	56	'Centennial Edition' of *Leaves of Grass*
1881	62	Seventh edition of *Leaves of Grass*, final arrangement of most of the poems
1882	62–3	*Specimen Days and Collect*. Threatened prosecution of *Leaves of Grass* for obscenity boosts sales and royalties
1884	65	Whitman now able to buy his own house in Camden
1888	69	Another paralytic stroke, and severe illness. *November Boughs*
1889	70	Eighth edition of *Leaves of Grass*
1891	72	'Authorized' or 'Deathbed' edition of *Leaves of Grass* (dated 1891–2)
1892	72	Whitman dies on 26 March. *Complete Prose Works*

Year	Literary Context	Historical Events
1858		Abraham Lincoln enters Senate as a Republican
1860		Nation linked by Morse's telegraph system
		Lincoln elected President
1861	Charles Dickens, *Great Expectations*	American Civil War begins
1863		Lincoln's Emancipation Proclamation
1865		Civil War ends
		Lincoln assassinated
1867		Alaska purchased from Russia
1868–9	Browning, *The Ring and the Book*	
1871–4	Eliot, *Middlemarch*	
1881	Henry James, *The Portrait of a Lady*	
1884	Mark Twain, *Adventures of Huckleberry Finn*	
1886	Death of Emily Dickinson	Chicago Foundation of the American Federation of Labor
1888	Edward Bellamy, *Looking Backward*	
1891	William James, *The Principles of Psychology*	